Claire
Macdonald
OF MACDONALD
Seasonal Cooking

CORGI BOOKS

A big thank you to Gog and the children for
being so long-suffering, Alyson Veitch (now
Hunter), Peter MacPherson who cooks here
with me, Minty Dallmeyer, and of course my
mother and sisters, Camilla and Olivia.

SEASONAL COOKING
A CORGI BOOK : 0 552 99804 4

Originally published in Great Britain by
Century Publishing Co Ltd

PRINTING HISTORY
Century edition published 1983
Corgi edition published 1986

15 17 19 20 18 16 14

This book is set in 11/12pt Baskerville.

Corgi Books are published by Transworld Publishers,
61–63 Uxbridge Road, London W5 5SA,
a division of The Random House Group Ltd,
in Australia by Random House Australia (Pty) Ltd,
20 Alfred Street, Milsons Point, Sydney, NSW 2061, Australia,
in New Zealand by Random House New Zealand Ltd,
18 Poland Road, Glenfield, Auckland 10, New Zealand
and in South Africa by Random House (Pty) Ltd,
Endulini, 5a Jubilee Road, Parktown 2193, South Africa.

Printed and bound in Great Britain by
Cox & Wyman Ltd, Reading, Berkshire.

Claire Macdonald and her husband run Kinloch Lodge Hotel on the Isle of Skye, which is also the family home for them and their four children. Claire is a well-known exponent of Scottish cooking and travels widely, lecturing and demonstrating recipes.

Introduction

When I married Godfrey, in 1969, he was a student chartered accountant and we set up home in Edinburgh. Within 18 months of our marriage his father died and Godfrey inherited the peerage and the High Chieftainship of the Clan Donald, the largest of the highland clans. Not long after this, circumstances dictated that we should leave Edinburgh and make our home and living in Skye, which now finds us running our own hotel, Kinloch Lodge.

At the time of writing our family consists of Alexandra, aged thirteen, Isabella, who is eleven, Meriel, who is eight, and Hugo, aged nearly five. We have recently built a wing on to Kinloch Lodge, having decided to sell our Ostaig house and make our home at Kinloch. It took ten years for us to reach the conclusion that life would be much easier all round if we lived over the shop, as it were, instead of 20 minutes' drive away. We will all see much more of each other and it is a beautiful, if rather remote, place in which to live.

When we took over Kinloch Lodge in 1974, neither of us had any training in hotel management. Godfrey had his accountant's apprenticeship, but I have never had any sort of training as a cook. The only thing we did have was a clear idea of the sort of holiday we would like ourselves if staying in a small hotel in the country. I don't feel we have achieved our ideal yet, not by a long way, but I hope that each year we get a bit closer to it. We aim for a comfortable, friendly, house-like sort of atmosphere.

The lodge itself helps. It was built in the early eighteenth century as a shooting lodge. It has always been a Macdonald house (part of the strategy for the battle of Culloden was plotted here) and for years it was let out for shooting parties. It became a hotel in 1952. There is a cosy feel about the house, with great open fires and the smell of wood smoke through the building. The elegant dining room has stunning views across Loch na Dal to the mountains of Knoydart on the mainland. Clan Donald portraits throughout the house keep visitors conscious of the history of the place and we use the family silver and lots of fresh and dried flowers to help keep the homey atmosphere.

Our visitors here have a comfortable life. They use the hotel as a centre for walking or exploring Skye by car, they sail and fish for brown trout in the lochs, they climb in the Cuillins or sit and read in front of the fire. The Clan Donald centre is only 12 miles to the south, where there is a museum with archives that help many overseas Macdonalds to trace their roots. The clan is an important part of our life and each year we meet many Macdonalds we've never met before.

When it comes to food in the hotel, breakfast is as important as dinner. We try to provide the sort of breakfast that Scotland used to be renowned for – a choice of fresh fruity concoctions, nourishing homemade muesli with yoghurt, porridge of course, plus good black pudding sausages, bacon, kidneys, eggs properly cooked and won-

8

derful kippers and we bake fresh scones each morning, so that they are warm from the oven for breakfast. After a breakfast like this, most guests feel they can dispense with even a light lunch.

Dinner is a far cry from the sameness of international hotel chain cooking. We try to achieve 'dinner party at home' sort of food – one's best home cooking every night. I am constantly thinking of new recipes, with inspiration coming from my mother, my sisters Camilla and Olivia, and special friends like Araminta Dallmeyer, April Strang Steel and Isabel Sydney, all of whom are very good cooks.

In this book there is a mixture of recipes that I serve at home and the sort of dishes that appear on the menu in the hotel. So there are the mundane but delicious Irish Stew with Black Pudding and Treacle Tart, alongside Smoked Haddock Roulade with Scallops and rich meringuey puds like Gâteau Diane. My intention is to share with you some of my favourite recipes, warning you of some of the pitfalls into which I have fallen along the way.

I cook mainly on an Aga, and would not be without it, but electric and gas settings are included for those who have more conventional cookers. I am also a staunch adherent of old-fashioned Imperial measurements, in lb, oz and pints – but for those younger than me who have learnt the metric system in school, metric equivalents are given alongside.

My cooking is always experimental because I am fascinated by food and love to eat. I do hope that others who feel this way will enjoy this book, both reading it and using the recipes.

January

I do wish that we in Britain celebrated Epiphany in the same way as the Italians do; then at least the twelve days of Christmas would end with a flourish. As it is, the Christmas holidays tend to drift on aimlessly once the excitement of Christmas is over. December 31st fills me with gloom. I can't think why I haven't adopted the Scots' great glee at the prospect of Hogmanay, but I haven't, so a day or so before New Year's Eve we – that is me, Godfrey and the children – head for my parents' home in North Lancashire. We stay there for several days, getting used to the New Year. Then we return home to Skye, and get on with January.

How I love the winters in Skye! As the autumn draws into winter, Skye reveals its true identity. There are virtually no visitors to the island, so nearly every car you meet on the road is a local car. I love having people to stay in our home at any time of the year, but best of all in the winter when we have time to enjoy them.

January is the month when I feel that I should be dieting off any Christmas excesses, and when I feel least inclined to do so. It is a month when I make lots of casseroles using all types of meat. January is also the peak month for citrus fruit. Traditionally, marmalade is made from Seville oranges, but there is a wide variety of citrus fruits to choose from – those interesting crosses between a grapefruit and an orange, for example, and the delicious clementine which far surpasses the rather dreary little satsuma. I experiment when making marmalade, using Seville oranges for half the quantity of fruit, and using a collection of other citrus fruit to make up the weight. It makes a different and less bitter marmalade.

First Courses

Apple, Chicory and Celery Salad with Tarragon Cream
Hot Cheesy Scones with Poppy Seeds
Artichoke Soup
Carrot and Coriander Soup
Pancakes Stuffed with Smoked Trout Pâté
Piperade with Garlic Fried Bread

Main Courses

Oxtail Stew
Steak and Kidney Pudding
Ragout of Lamb with Red Wine
Beef Casserole with Beer and Onions
Chicken, Leek and Parsley Pie

Vegetables

Cabbage Fried with Grainy Mustard
Bashed Neeps

Desserts

Clementine Soufflé
Treacle Tart
Pavlova with Lemon Curd and Cream
Pears in Fudge Sauce
Toasted Coconut Ice Cream with Hot Brandy and Orange
Mincemeat Sauce

Preserves

Marmalade

Apple, Chicory & Celery Salad with Tarragon Cream

This salad makes a delicious first course in the winter months. Use a good eating apple like Cox's Orange Pippin. I leave the skins on, but you may prefer to peel them.

Serves 6

---

*3 eating apples, cored and
    cut into smallish pieces*
*3 heads of chicory, cut into
    1 in (2.5 cm) lengths*

*6 sticks of celery, very finely
    sliced*
*Tarragon Cream, see pages
    126–7, 222–3*

Mix the apples, chicory and celery together in a bowl and stir in the tarragon cream until everything is well blended. Serve on small plates accompanied by Hot Cheesy Scones with Poppy Seeds.

Hot Cheesy Scones with Poppy Seeds

Makes 9

---

*12 oz (350 g) self-raising
    flour*
½ rounded teaspoon salt
*1 rounded teaspoon baking
    powder*
*2 rounded teaspoons mustard
    powder*
*1 egg, beaten with 1
    tablespoon sunflower seed
    oil*

*just less than ½ pint
    (300 ml) milk*
*4 oz (125 g) strong Cheddar
    cheese, grated*
*1 rounded tablespoon poppy
    seeds*

Sieve the dry ingredients into a bowl and stir in the egg, oil and milk. Add the cheese and knead all the ingredients together well – it will be a rather sticky mixture.

Pat the mixture out on a well-floured surface, to a thickness of about 1 in (2.5 cm). Using a floured 2½ in (6 cm) cutter, cut the scones into circles and put them on a baking tray, sprinkling the surface of each with poppy seeds. Bake in a hot oven, 425°F (220°C) Gas Mark 7 (the top right-hand oven in a 4-door Aga) for 10–15 minutes, until they are well risen and golden brown. Serve the scones warm. You can mix all the dry ingredients in advance, ready to add the egg and milk and pop them into the oven at the last minute.

Artichoke Soup

The Jerusalem artichoke is a winter vegetable which grows like a weed and has one of the most subtle flavours I know; I find people either love it or loathe it. These lovely vegetables are rather knobbly and so a fiddle to peel, but worth every minute of the time it takes. They make a most delicious simple soup, which also freezes well.

Serves 6

---

2 oz (50 g) butter
1 onion, peeled and chopped
1 lb (450 g) Jerusalem artichokes, peeled and roughly chopped
2 pints (1.1 litres) chicken stock

salt and freshly ground black pepper
6 tablespoons single cream
finely chopped parsley or chives

Melt the butter in a saucepan, add the onion and cook over a gentle heat, stirring from time to time, until the onion is

14

soft and transparent. Add the chopped artichokes, cook for a minute or two, then pour on the stock. Bring to the boil, cover the pan and simmer gently for 30 minutes.

Remove from the heat, cool and purée in a blender. Season and reheat to serve. Just before dishing up the soup, add a spoonful of single cream and some finely chopped parsley or chives to each plateful.

Carrot & Coriander Soup

Carrots are wonderful either raw, or cooked as a vegetable, or as a soup. This is an easy, low-calorie soup. Coriander goes well with carrots; if you haven't come across it before, and are uncertain how much you like, just put less in the first time.

Serves 6

---

2 oz (50 g) butter
1 large onion, peeled and finely chopped
4 large carrots, peeled and chopped
1 potato, peeled and chopped

2 rounded dessertspoons coriander seeds
2 pints (1.1 litres) chicken stock
salt and freshly ground black pepper
a little finely chopped parsley

Melt the butter in a saucepan on a low heat. Add the chopped onion and cook until it is soft. Stir in the carrots, potato and coriander. Cook, stirring from time to time, for about 5 minutes.

Pour on the stock and season with a little salt and black pepper. Bring to the boil, cover the saucepan and simmer very gently for 30–40 minutes, or until the vegetables are soft. Let it cool slightly, purée the soup in a blender and then sieve it. You need to sieve this soup because the blender doesn't break down the coriander seeds. Actually I rather like the bits of coriander you get if you don't sieve the soup, but Godfrey says they are like toenails so I feel that for everyone else's benefit I have to sieve it!

Reheat to serve, and just before dishing up stir some finely chopped parsley through the soup.

Pancakes Stuffed with Smoked Trout Pâté

It is worth hunting out fresh smoked trout as frozen ones, while better than nothing, tend to be rather watery. We get wonderful smoked trout for use at Kinloch.

Serves 8

---

4 small smoked trout
8 oz (225 g) cream cheese
2 tablespoons lemon juice
 (you may want to add
 more, if you prefer a more
 lemony flavour)
1 rounded teaspoon
 horseradish sauce
freshly ground black pepper
16 pancakes, see page 58

finely chopped parsley
For Sour Cream and
 Cucumber Sauce:
½ cucumber, peeled
¼ pint (150 ml) sour cream
¼ pint (150 ml) single
 cream
a little salt
freshly ground black pepper

Carefully take the skin off the smoked trout and remove the bones. Put the flesh, the cream cheese, lemon juice, horseradish and black pepper into a food processor, and whizz until well blended. If you haven't got a food processor, you can do this in small quantities in a blender, or pound and mash the ingredients together in a bowl, using the end of a rolling pin; but however hard you work at it, this method will not produce as smooth a result as you

16

will get from a food processor. Divide the pâté between the pancakes, and roll them up. Arrange the pancakes on a large plate (what we call an ashet in Scotland).

Using a teaspoon, scoop out the cucumber seeds. Dice the flesh and set aside in a small bowl.

If you, like me, cannot buy commercially soured cream, use ¼ pint (150 ml) double cream and sour it with 1 tablespoon lemon juice.

Stir the two creams together, with the seasoning. Just before serving the pancakes, add the diced cucumber to the cream and pour the sauce over the rolled-up pancakes. Sprinkle with finely chopped parsley.

Piperade with Garlic Fried Bread

This is an eggy dish which can be used as a first course, or makes an excellent main course for supper. It is a recipe for those who, like me, love garlic; it is good served with triangles of fried bread.

Serves 6

2 tablespoons olive oil	*or 2 fresh red peppers,*
2 oz (50 g) butter	*seeded and finely sliced*
2 medium-sized onions,	*12 eggs, beaten together*
peeled and thinly sliced	*salt and freshly ground black*
1 garlic clove, peeled and	*pepper*
finely chopped	*6 slices fried bread*
5 oz (140 g) tin pimentos,	*finely chopped parsley,*
drained and finely sliced,	*optional*

Heat the olive oil in a saucepan and melt the butter in the oil. Put the onions, garlic and red peppers in the pan (if you are using fresh peppers). Cook over a gentle heat until the onions and peppers are soft and the onions look

17

transparent. If you are using tinned pimentos, add them to the saucepan at this stage, when the onions are cooked.

Add the beaten eggs and stir over a gentle heat until they are scrambled. This must be done at the last minute, but you can cook the onion and pepper mixture ahead, and add the beaten eggs to finish off the dish just before serving.

Season with salt and freshly ground black pepper, and pile the piperade in a shallow serving dish, arranging the fried bread around the edge of the eggs. If you have any to hand, sprinkle some finely chopped parsley over the top before serving.

If you have an Aga, you can fry the bread (and I like to add a clove of garlic to the oil) up to 2 hours beforehand, and keep it warm. Put it on a plate lined with kitchen paper to drain off the excess fat.

Oxtail Stew

My favourite of all casseroles is Oxtail Stew, perfect for Januarys. One thing I have learnt is that oxtails are not good when frozen raw, so do beware the frozen packages of oxtails which are to be found conveniently stacked in most butchers' deep freezes. The cooked casserole, on the other hand, freezes perfectly well, but not for too long – I wouldn't leave an oxtail stew in the deep freeze for much more than a month.

The secret of oxtail stew lies in the long cooking time. It should be cooked until the meat is literally falling off the bones. As I have a 4-door Aga, I can cook a stew like this overnight, barely simmering, and this is the best sort of cooking it can have.

Serves 6–8, depending on the size of the oxtails

2 oxtails
4 tablespoons sunflower seed
oil
3 medium-sized onions,
peeled and thinly sliced
6 carrots, peeled and cut into
fine strips
½ small turnip, peeled and
cut into fine strips about
the same size as the
carrots

1 clove of garlic, peeled and
finely chopped
2 rounded tablespoons plain
flour
¾ pint (425 ml) cider or pale
ale
2 rounded tablespoons tomato
purée
bouquet garni
salt and freshly ground black
pepper

Cut up the oxtails, trimming each piece of as much surplus fat as possible. Heat the oil in a large flameproof casserole which has a close-fitting lid. Brown the pieces of oxtail well all over in the hot fat. Part of the success of a good casserole depends on browning the meat well and to do this you can only brown a few pieces at a time, otherwise the fat loses heat and the meat turns greyish and tends to stew in its juices rather than brown. As the pieces of oxtail brown, remove them to a separate dish and keep them warm.

Lower the heat under the casserole and add the onions to the fat. Cook gently until they are soft and transparent – they shouldn't turn brown. Next add the carrots, turnip and garlic and cook, still over a gentle to moderate heat, for 5 minutes, stirring from time to time. Sprinkle over the flour and cook for 2 minutes, scraping the bottom of the pan. Gradually add the cider or ale, the tomato purée and 1 pint (600 ml) water, stirring all the time until the sauce boils. Put in the bouquet garni and season with salt and pepper.

Return the pieces of oxtail to the casserole, cover with a piece of foil and then put the lid on top. Cook in a low oven, 250°F (130°C) Gas Mark ½ for about 3 hours. If using an

Aga, cook for 1 hour in the bottom right-hand oven, then transfer to the top left-hand oven for 2 hours.

Leave the casserole to cool, preferably overnight, and when quite cold, skim any fat from the surface. You may need to add another ½ pint (300 ml) water at this stage if the gravy looks too thick for your liking.

Re-cover the casserole and cook at 250°F (130°C) Gas Mark ½ (top left-hand oven in a 4-door Aga) for a good 2 hours, preferably more. Remove the bouquet garni and serve with creamy mashed potatoes and a green vegetable.

Steak & Kidney Pudding

So many people go into raptures over a steak and kidney pudding that I can't think why I don't make it more often. It must be the most comforting dish of all to eat on a cold winter's day. I always put mushrooms in mine, because they have a real affinity with steak and kidney.

For casseroles, puddings and braised dishes I use a lean braising steak that in this part of Scotland is known as rump; in other parts of Britain it would be called topside or silverside.

Serves 6

12 oz (350 g) self-raising flour

6 oz (175 g) shredded suet

2 rounded tablespoons finely chopped parsley, optional

salt and freshly ground black pepper

1½ lb (675 g) beef, cut into 1 in (2.5 cm) cubes

8 oz (225 g) ox kidney, trimmed and cut into smaller cubes than the beef

2 rounded tablespoons plain flour seasoned with salt and freshly ground black pepper

8 oz (225 g) mushrooms, wiped, with their stalks removed and sliced

Mix together the flour, suet, parsley (if using) and seasoning and stir in enough cold water to make a soft, pliable dough. Cut off about a quarter of the dough and roll out the remainder to line a buttered 3 pint (1.7 litre) pudding basin. Roll out the separate quarter, which will make the lid of the pudding.

Roll the cubes of beef and kidney in the seasoned flour. Pack the meat and kidney and sliced mushrooms into the dough-lined pudding basin, fill almost to the top with cold water and place the lid on top. Trim it to fit, allowing enough to pinch together with the dough lining the basin.

Cover the pudding with a layer of buttered greaseproof paper and then a layer of foil, about 2 in (5 cm) larger in circumference than the top of the pudding, and pleat it once in the middle. This pleat allows for expansion during cooking. Tie the foil tightly around the pudding basin with fine string, and put the pudding in a large saucepan. Fill the saucepan about half full with boiling water, cover with a lid, and simmer the pudding for about 6 hours, taking care not to let the water boil away – top up if necessary. To serve, remove the foil and greaseproof paper from the top, wipe the basin as clean as you can and tie a table napkin round it.

If you want to cook the pudding a day ahead, let it cool completely and refrigerate overnight. To reheat just put the pudding in a pan of boiling water, cover and simmer for $1\frac{1}{2}$–2 hours.

Ragout of Lamb with Red Wine

This is a recipe which was given to me by my mother. It is quite delicious, easy to make, and will freeze though not for much more than a month. The most arduous part of making this lamb ragout is peeling the small onions, but this task is made much easier by pouring boiling water over them for a few minutes first – their skins then slip off, thereby reducing the crying time considerably. I find, incidentally, that wearing contact lenses helps to prevent the onion fumes from making my eyes stream.

Serves 6

---

2 lb (900 g) boneless leg of
    lamb, cut into 1 in
    (2.5 cm) cubes
8 oz (225 g) unsmoked
    bacon, as lean as possible,
    cut into 1 in (2.5 cm)
    cubes
2 oz (50 g) butter
18 tiny onions, peeled

3 rounded tablespoons plain
    flour
¾ pint (450 ml) red wine
bouquet garni
12 oz (350 g) mushrooms,
    sliced
salt and freshly ground black
    pepper

Melt the butter in a flameproof casserole, add the lamb and the bacon a few pieces at a time and cook until they are well browned all over. Remove from the pan to a separate dish and keep warm. Lower the heat slightly and add the onions. Cook gently, shaking the pan occasionally, until the onions are golden. Sprinkle in the flour, stir well and cook for a further 2–3 minutes. Then gradually add ½ pint (300 ml) water and the wine, stirring all the time until the sauce boils.

Replace the meat in the casserole, and add the bouquet garni and the mushrooms, salt and pepper. Cover tightly, and cook in a moderate oven, 350°F (180°C) Gas Mark 4 (the bottom right-hand oven in a 4-door Aga) for 1½ hours. Remove the bouquet garni before serving.

Beef Casserole with Beer & Onions

This is a good dish for an informal party in the winter. The secret of success with this recipe lies in browning the meat really well all over. If possible, make this the day before it is needed, leave overnight, and reheat in a moderate oven for 45 minutes. It is good served with baked potatoes, and with cabbage fried with butter and grainy mustard, as much or as little mustard as you like (see page 26).

Serves 6

2½ lb (1.2 kg) lean braising beef, cut into 1½ in (4 cm) cubes
2 tablespoons oil
1 oz (25 g) butter
4 onions, peeled and thinly sliced
1 clove of garlic, peeled and finely chopped

1 rounded teaspoon sugar
1 heaped tablespoon plain flour
¾ pint (425 ml) beer
bouquet garni
salt and freshly ground black pepper

Heat the oil and butter together in a flameproof casserole. Add the meat, a little at a time, and cook until well browned all over. Remove the meat to a separate dish and keep warm.

Lower the heat, add the onions and garlic to the pan, and cook, stirring from time to time, until the onions are soft and transparent. Sprinkle over the sugar, and cook for a further minute, then stir in the flour. Cook for another couple of minutes, then gradually pour on the beer and ½ pint (300 ml) water, stirring all the time until the sauce boils.

Add the bouquet garni and seasoning to the pan, replace the meat in it, cover with a lid, and cook in a slow to moderate oven, 325°F (170°C) Gas Mark 3 (bottom right-hand oven in a 4-door Aga) for 1½ hours. Remove the bouquet garni before serving.

Chicken, Leek & Parsley Pie

This is a marvellous pie, extremely popular with adults and children alike.

Serves 8

---

1 large chicken, about 4½ lb (2 kg)
2 onions, peeled
1 carrot, peeled and cut in chunks
bouquet garni
salt
a few black peppercorns
3 oz (75 g) butter
4 good-sized leeks, washed, trimmed and cut into ½ in (1 cm) pieces

1 rounded teaspoon curry powder
2 oz (50 g) plain flour
1 pint (568 ml) milk
½ pint (300 ml) chicken stock
freshly ground black pepper
2 rounded tablespoons finely chopped parsley
12 oz (350 g) puff pastry
milk for glazing

Put the chicken in a large saucepan and cover with water. Add 1 onion, cut in quarters, the carrot chunks, bouquet garni, salt and peppercorns. Bring to the boil, cover with a lid and simmer gently for 1 hour or until the juices run clear when the point of a knife is stuck into the chicken thigh. Cool the chicken in the stock in which it cooked. When cool, strip all the meat from the bones, and put in a deep 3½ pint (2 litre) pie dish. Finely chop the remaining onion.

24

Melt the butter in a saucepan. Add the sliced leeks and the chopped onion and cook gently for about 10 minutes, when the onions should be soft and transparent. Stir in the curry powder and the flour. Cook for 1–2 minutes longer, then gradually stir in the milk and the chicken stock, stirring until the sauce boils. Season with salt and pepper. Stir in the finely chopped parsley. Pour over the chicken meat in the pie dish, and mix well.

Roll out the puff pastry, and use it to cover the pie. Decorate the pie with pastry leaves and brush the surface all over with milk. Bake in a hot oven 425°F (220°C) Gas Mark 7 (top right-hand oven in a 4-door Aga) for 20 minutes, then lower the heat to 350°F (180°C) Gas Mark 4 (bottom right-hand oven in a 4-door Aga) for a further 20 minutes, or until the pie is golden brown.

Cabbage Fried with Grainy Mustard

Cabbage is one of those things which conjures up in people's minds awful visions of greatly over-cooked mush in a pool of water, with that all-pervading smell which seemed to fill the sort of institution which turned out cabbage like this. Poor cabbage, because it is a delicious winter vegetable, and can be cooked in a number of ways. I think it is very complementary to stewey dishes. This is one of my favourite ways of cooking and eating cabbage.

Serves 6

about ½ a large cabbage
3 oz (75 g) butter
2 rounded tablespoons grainy mustard, such as Meaux

salt and freshly ground black pepper

Shred the cabbage finely. Melt the butter in a wide, shallow pan, and stir the mustard into it, then add the cabbage. Cook over a gentle heat, stirring occasionally, for up to 30 minutes; how long you cook it depends on how crunchy you like to eat cabbage.

Bashed Neeps

This is a traditional Scottish dish which is simply mashed turnips. Traditionally they go with haggis and are eaten on Burns Night, towards the end of January. Burns Night celebrations make me feel decidedly English because I do not like haggis and I'm not very fond of Burns either. The one redeeming feature of Burns Night is, for me, the mashed turnips. They are delicious, mashed together with lots of butter and black pepper.

Clementine Soufflé

Lemon soufflé is always a popular dessert, providing that it is very lemony, not too gelatinous and with a lovely creamy texture. A soufflé flavoured with clementines and just a little lemon makes a change; it takes advantage of the delicious fruit which are so plentiful at this time of year.

Serves 6

---

grated rind and juice of 1
  lemon
juice of 2 clementines
½ level tablespoon gelatine
4 large eggs, separated

6 oz (175 g) caster sugar
grated rind of 3 clementines
7 fl oz (200 ml) double
  cream, whipped

Put the squeezed juices of the lemon and 2 clementines in a small saucepan and sprinkle the gelatine on the juice. Let it soak in, then put the pan over a very low heat until the gelatine is dissolved. Remove from the heat.

Beat the egg yolks, gradually adding the caster sugar, and beat together until thick and pale. Stir the grated rind of the lemon and 3 clementines into the whipped cream. Stir the dissolved gelatine into the yolk and sugar mixture and fold in the whipped cream. Leave until starting to set.

Whisk the egg whites until stiff, and when the cream and egg yolk mixture is set enough to thickly coat the back of a spoon, fold the whites into it, using a metal spoon. Pour the soufflé mixture into a glass or china serving dish and chill until set.

Treacle Tart

When the old-fashioned English recipes appear on a table they are generally much appreciated. People just don't make and eat puddings like they used to – we are all too conscious of our weight – but I am sure that if our consciences permitted us we would eat many more like this one.

Serves 6–8

---

12 oz (350 g) shortcrust
pastry
8 tablespoons golden syrup
3 oz (75 g) butter

3 small or 2 large eggs,
beaten
whipped cream, to serve

Roll out the pastry to line a flan dish measuring about 9 in (23 cm) in diameter. Prick the base with a fork, and put the dish in the refrigerator for 30 minutes. Then bake blind in a moderate oven, 350°F (180°C) Gas Mark 4 (bottom right-hand oven in a 4-door Aga) for 20 minutes, until the pastry is cooked.

Measure the 8 tablespoons of golden syrup into a saucepan. This can be a sticky job, but if you have a small saucepan of boiling water and dip the tablespoon into the boiling water before the first spoonful of syrup is taken from the tin, and in between each spoonful, the syrup will slide quite easily off the hot spoon into the saucepan.

Warm the syrup until it is runny, then beat in the butter, a bit at a time, until it is all melted. Next, beat in the beaten eggs. Pour this into the cooked pastry case, and bake in a moderate oven, 350°F (180°C) Gas Mark 4 (bottom right-hand oven in a 4-door Aga) for 25 minutes, or until the filling is just firm to the touch. Serve the treacle tart warm or cold, with whipped but unsweetened cream.

Pavlova with Lemon Curd & Cream

I do love the vanilla flavour and marshmallow-like consistency of pavlovas. They take only a few minutes to make, and about 1 hour to cook, and they are so versatile, because you can fill them with any fruit mixed with whipped cream. This month, to take advantage of citrus fruits being at their peak, I suggest a filling of freshly made lemon curd mixed with the whipped cream. If you would rather, you can spread the lemon curd on the surface of the pavlova and cover it with whipped cream.

Serves 6–8

4 egg whites
8 oz (225 g) caster sugar
1 rounded teaspoon cornflour, sieved
1 teaspoon wine vinegar
1 teaspoon vanilla essence
½ pint (300 ml) double cream

For the lemon curd:
grated rind and juice of 3 lemons
3 oz (75 g) butter
12 oz (350 g) caster sugar
2 whole eggs
2 egg yolks

Make the lemon curd first. Put the grated lemon rinds and juice, butter and sugar together either in a double saucepan over simmering water, or in a heavy-bottomed saucepan over a gentle heat. Stir the mixture occasionally, until the sugar has completely dissolved.

Beat together the eggs and the yolks until well mixed, then pour a little of the hot lemon mixture on to the eggs. Mix well, and pour the egg mixture into the pan with the rest of the lemon, sugar and butter mixture. Over a gentle heat, and stirring continuously, cook until the mixture thickens. Do not let it boil. Remove from the heat, and put into jars – this quantity will fill two 1 lb (450 g) jars or rather less. You will only need one jar for the pavlova, so eat the contents of the other jar for tea.

To make the pavlova, whisk the egg whites until stiff. Start adding the caster sugar to them gradually, when they are nearly stiff, and whisk the whole lot in bit by bit. Quickly, using a metal spoon, fold in the sieved cornflour, the vinegar and the vanilla essence.

Spread a piece of siliconised paper on a baking sheet and tip the pavlova mixture on to it. Shape the pavlova into an oval, hollowing out the centre and building up the sides as much as you can. Bake in a moderate oven, 350°F (180°C) Gas Mark 4 (bottom right-hand oven in a 4-door Aga) for 5 minutes, then lower the heat to 250°F (130°C) Gas Mark ½ (top left-hand oven in the Aga) and bake for 1 hour.

Remove from the oven, cool, then turn on to a serving dish. The hollow bit will sink, so that you still have an indentation in the middle.

Whip the double cream until quite stiff, fold into it 1 lb (450 g) lemon curd and pile up on top of the pavlova. Or alternatively spread the lemon curd over the pavlova and cover with the whipped cream.

Pears in Fudge Sauce

This is the most delicious pud. It is dead easy to make and the idea came to me one evening in an unaccustomed flash of inspiration as I gazed at some pears wondering what to do with them for dinner. The sauce is also delicious with vanilla ice cream and, if you have some left over, it keeps well in a screw-top jar in the refrigerator for several days.

Serves 6 generously, or 8 if following a filling first course

---

9 pears (8 if they are very large)
4 oz (125 g) butter

6 oz (175 g) soft brown sugar, dark or light
7 fl oz (225 ml) double cream

Put the butter, sugar and cream together in a saucepan; heat gently, stirring, until the butter is melted and the sugar completely dissolved. Then boil gently over a steady heat, for a good 5 minutes.

Meanwhile peel and core the pears and cut into quarters. Put the pear quarters in a shallow dish. (It doesn't matter if they go a bit brown.) Cool the sauce a little, then pour over the pears. Serve at once.

Toasted Coconut Ice Cream with Hot Brandy & Orange Mincemeat Sauce

This is a lovely dessert for a winter's evening, the sauce warms you from the inside out!

Serves 8

---

4 eggs, separated
4 oz (125 g) icing sugar, sieved
½ pint (300 ml) double cream, whipped
3 rounded tablespoons desiccated coconut, toasted

until golden brown, then cooled

For the sauce:
8 oz (225 g) mincemeat
grated rind of 1 orange
3 tablespoons brandy

Whisk the egg whites until they are quite stiff then add the sieved icing sugar, spoonful by spoonful, whisking all the time. In a separate bowl, beat the yolks until smooth then fold them into the whipped cream. Fold the cream and yolk mixture into the egg white mixture, alternately with the cooled, toasted coconut. Put the ice cream mixture into a polythene container with a lid, and freeze. You do not need to beat this ice cream as it freezes, but take it out of the deep freeze 20 minutes before you want to eat it.

To make the sauce, put all the ingredients together in a saucepan, and stir over a gentle heat. Don't let it boil. Serve the sauce hot, with the ice cream.

Marmalade

Marmalade is a very personal taste; some people like it rather bitter and chunky while others prefer it to be sweeter, more jellied than syrupy, and with the fruit cut more finely. I find that each year my marmalade varies a little. We make gallons of marmalade at Kinloch, and there is great satisfaction, I find, in going into the larder to gaze at the rows of jars.

This is the basic recipe that I follow each year. The citrus fruit other than Seville oranges varies from year to year and from one marmalade-making session to the next, but I prefer not to use satsumas.

Makes 11–12 lb (5–5.4 kg)

1½ lb (700 g) Seville oranges
1½ lb (700 g) other citrus fruit – perhaps a grapefruit, a sweet orange, and the balance of

the weight made up with good-tasting tangerines or clementines
6 lb (2.75 kg) granulated or preserving sugar

Put the fruit in a large saucepan or jam pan with 4 pints (2.3 litres) water, and simmer gently for about 6 hours – I put mine in the top left-hand oven of my 4-door Aga overnight.

Remove the fruit from the water in the pan and cut each orange, tangerine or grapefruit in half. Scoop out all the pips into a small saucepan, cover with ½ pint (300 ml) water and simmer for 10 minutes. Leave to cool, then strain this liquid into the jam pan with the water the fruit was cooked in.

While the pips are simmering, cut up the fruit – I put mine in a food processor. Put the cut-up fruit back in the water in the jam pan. Add the sugar and cook on a low heat, stirring occasionally until the sugar has completely dissolved. Then boil furiously, and after 10 minutes pull the pan off the heat to test whether the marmalade is setting. Do this by dripping some of the hot marmalade on to a cold saucer (I put a saucer in the refrigerator); leave it for a few minutes and if, when you push the surface of the sample with the tip of your finger, the skin on top of the marmalade wrinkles, you have a set. If it is still runny, put the jam pan back on the heat, boil vigorously for a further 5 minutes and test again. Always remember to pull the pan off the heat while testing for a set, otherwise it may go too far.

Pot when still hot into warmed jars, and cover with a circle of waxed paper. Seal completely with cellophane and rubber bands when quite cold.

February

February is the month in Skye when spring seems a distinct possibility. The evenings begin to be noticeably lighter, and the snowdrops, the first of our wonderful spring wild flowers, appear. We have some of the best weather of the year in February: in fact one year we had a picnic in February on the beach at the bottom of our garden, looking across the Sound of Sleat to the snow-topped mountains, beautiful against the blue sky.

February is the last month of our working winter. This month we have to start trying to find the right people to pad out the nucleus of local staff we are lucky enough to have at Kinloch Lodge. To me and to our staff the glow of satisfaction comes with guests who express their appreciation of the food and service they receive. Some even write to thank us, and these letters we pin to the noticeboard in the kitchen at Kinloch. It is for people who will join in our eagerness to provide a welcome that we have to search each season.

When we first came to live permanently in Skye, the choice of vegetables available was minimal. Each year the situation has changed, thanks to the awareness of our local shopkeepers to public demand for a wider variety of fresh fruit and vegetables. In February they are mostly root vegetables, with the exception of leeks, cabbage and Brussels sprouts. But they all, in their various guises, complement well the winter stews, casseroles and game dishes.

First Courses

Creamy Smoked Haddock Soup
Leek and Potato Soup
Leeks Vinaigrette
Celeriac Mayonnaise

Main Courses

Parsley Omelette with Chopped Ham
Creamy Leek Puffed Pastry Pie
Pot Roast of Beef with Oranges
Mushroom, Cheese and Garlic Soufflé
Pigeon and Steak Pie

Vegetables

Artichokes as a Vegetable
Parsnips
Parsnip and Carrot Ragout
Crunchy Tops for Vegetables

Desserts

Carrot Cake
Pear and Ginger Mousse
Apple Pie

Creamy Smoked Haddock Soup

This is a traditional Scottish soup, called Cullen Skink. It is exquisitely flavoured, simple to make and greatly enjoyed by all who like fish.

Serves 6

$1\frac{1}{2}$ lb (700 g) smoked
   haddock
2 pints (1.1 litres) milk and
   water mixed
2 onions, peeled
1 blade of mace
2 oz (50 g) butter
3 medium-sized potatoes,
   peeled and chopped

2 tomatoes, skinned, seeded
   and chopped
freshly ground black pepper
1 rounded tablespoon finely
   chopped parsley
12 dessertspoons single
   cream
chopped parsley or chives, to
   garnish

Put the fish in a saucepan and cover with the milk and water; add a whole onion and the mace. Over a gentle heat bring slowly to the boil, simmer very gently for barely 5 minutes, then remove from the heat and leave to stand for 10 minutes. Strain off the liquid.

Chop the second onion. In another saucepan, melt the butter, add the chopped potatoes and onion, and cook for about 10 minutes over a gentle heat, stirring from time to time, until the onion begins to soften. Pour on the strained fish liquid and simmer gently until the pieces of potato are soft. Remove from the heat, cool and purée in a blender.

Rinse out the saucepan. Put the puréed soup into it. Flake the cooked fish, being careful to remove all bones and skin, and stir the fish into the soup. Stir in the chopped tomatoes and black pepper to taste and reheat gently. Add the finely chopped parsley just before serving. Into each plateful of soup put 2 dessertspoons of cream and sprinkle with a little more parsley, or chives, to garnish.

Leek & Potato Soup

It is imperative to make soup from good stock. You can substitute water and chicken stock cubes if you must, but the end result will be much inferior in taste and, curiously enough, in texture too.

Leek and potato soup is warming and quite filling, as are most soups, but not very high in calories, being made purely from vegetables. I like to put some curry powder in, but not enough to make one recognise its presence, just enough to give it a sort of glow. Leek and potato soup becomes vichyssoise when it is served cold, smooth and delicious with cream and chives on top.

Serves 6–8

2 oz (50 g) butter
1 large onion, peeled and chopped
6 good-sized leeks – more if they are the small, thin leeks – washed and cut into pieces about 1 in (2.5 cm) long
1 stick celery, chopped, optional

3 medium-sized potatoes, peeled and chopped
1 rounded dessertspoon curry powder
2 pints (1.1 litres) chicken stock
salt and freshly ground black pepper

Melt the butter in a saucepan, add the chopped onion and cook gently for about 10 minutes, until the onion is soft and transparent. Then add the sliced leeks, chopped celery and potatoes and cook for a further 4–5 minutes, stirring from time to time.

Stir in the curry powder, cook for 1–2 minutes more and then pour in the stock. Bring the contents of the saucepan to the boil then simmer gently for 30–45 minutes, until the potato is cooked. Remove the pan from the heat, cool and purée in a blender. Season to taste and reheat to serve.

If the celery looks as though it might be even slightly stringy, sieve the puréed soup, as you don't want anything to detract from the velvety smoothness.

Leeks Vinaigrette

Leeks can be the answer to a winter salad. This recipe is so easy, and can be served as a salad accompanying a main course, or it can be a first course, served with warm wholemeal rolls.

Serves 6

---

12 medium-sized leeks, washed and trimmed of any tough outer leaves, but left whole
salt

about 4 tablespoons French dressing, see page 130
1 rounded tablespoon finely chopped parsley

Simmer the leeks in salted water for about 15 minutes, until they are just tender when you push the point of a knife in. Drain well, arrange them in a shallow dish, and while they are still warm cover with French dressing, mixing it in to coat each leek. Sprinkle with the chopped parsley and serve when cold.

Celeriac Mayonnaise

Celeriac has a distinct flavour that combines well with other root vegetables, such as potatoes or carrots in a mixed purée. This is a cold dish making a delicious winter salad.

3 roots of celeriac, washed, peeled, and cut into fine strips	*finely chopped parsley*
	about 4 tablespoons
	mayonnaise, see page 128
salt	

Simmer the strips of celeriac in salted water for 10 minutes until they are just soft, but not breaking up. Drain well. Mix 1 tablespoon finely chopped parsley into the mayonnaise and fold in the celeriac strips. Pile in a shallow serving dish, and sprinkle with more finely chopped parsley.

As with the leeks vinaigrette, this can be eaten as either a side-salad or as a first course.

Parsley Omelette with Chopped Ham

Omelettes are very satisfying. They can be served folded over their filling or, as in Omelette Arnold Bennett, served flat with their creamy filling covering their surface. This omelette has lots of parsley in the egg mixture, which looks pretty and tastes good.

For each person:	*1 rounded dessertspoon finely*
2 eggs, beaten	*chopped parsley*
salt, pepper and a dash of	*½ oz (15 g) butter*
Tabasco	*2 oz (50 g) chopped ham*

Beat together the eggs, 1 tablespoon cold water, the seasoning and parsley. In an omelette pan (which should never be washed, just wiped out thoroughly with kitchen paper whilst still warm) melt ½ oz (15 g) butter. When the butter is foaming, pour in the egg and parsley mixture.

Cook over a medium heat, lifting the edges of the omelette from time to time to allow the runny mixture to go underneath. When the omelette is still slightly uncooked on top, sprinkle the chopped ham over the surface. Cook a minute or two longer, then fold over and slip on to a warmed plate.

Omelettes are best eaten straight away, but this isn't very sociable. They will keep warm perfectly well in the time it takes to make omelettes for 4 people. Serve with warm Brown Garlic Rolls (see page 143) and a green salad, and there you have one of the simplest and best meals.

Creamy Leek Puffed Pastry Pie

We make this recipe for a first course at the Kinloch Hotel, and at home we have it for a main course lunch or supper dish. You can adapt it to use up leftover chopped ham or chicken, or have it simply as the recipe goes, served with a green salad. Bought made-up puff pastry is excellent. I prefer to cook the pie in a tin rather than a china flan dish, as the pastry cooks better.

Serves 8 as a first course; 6 as a main course

---

1 lb (450 g) puff pastry
3 oz (75 g) butter
8 good-sized leeks, well washed and cut into pieces about 1 in (2.5 cm) long
4 fairly heaped tablespoons plain flour

1 pint (570 ml) milk
salt and freshly ground black pepper
2 pinches nutmeg, preferably freshly grated
2 egg yolks
milk for glazing

Roll out half the pastry and use it to line an 8–9 in (20–23 cm) flan tin. Prick the base and chill while you

42

prepare the filling. Melt the butter in a saucepan, add the chopped leeks and cook gently for about 10 minutes, stirring from time to time, until the leeks are soft. Stir in the flour, cook for a couple of minutes, then gradually stir in the milk, stirring until the mixture boils. Season with salt, freshly ground black pepper and nutmeg, and draw off the heat.

In a small bowl mix the 2 egg yolks together well, and add a little of the hot sauce from the saucepan to the yolks; mix together well, then pour the contents of the bowl into the saucepan and stir until thoroughly mixed. Leave to cool.

Pour the filling into the puff pastry case. Roll out the remaining pastry and cover the pie, pinching the edges together neatly and slashing the surface in 2–3 places to let the steam out during cooking. Brush the surface of the pastry with milk, and bake in a hot oven, 425°F (220°C) Gas Mark 7 (the bottom of the top right-hand oven in a 4-door Aga) for about 30 minutes, until the pie is golden brown and risen. Serve immediately.

Pot Roast of Beef with Oranges

I love a pot roast, chiefly for its flavour but also for its convenience. It really has to be made the day before it is required, and all it needs to accompany it is either creamy mashed potatoes or baked potatoes. This recipe is slightly different and is ideal for winter, when citrus fruit is at its best, as it has oranges in the ingredients.

Serves 6–8

---

1 oz (25 g) butter
1 tablespoon sunflower seed oil
3 lb (1.4 kg) brisket of beef
6 medium-sized onions, peeled and thinly sliced
4 carrots, peeled and cut into fine strips
1 clove of garlic, peeled and finely chopped

2 tablespoons tomato purée
1 rounded tablespoon plain flour
2 oranges, peeled and sliced
2 cloves
1 bayleaf
salt and freshly ground black pepper

Heat the butter and oil in a heavy flameproof casserole which has a tight-fitting lid. Brown the brisket well on all sides, then remove and keep warm. Put the sliced onions, carrots and garlic in the pan and, over a fairly gentle heat, cook until the onions are beginning to soften. Add the tomato purée and the flour to the pan, and stir well in and cook for 2–3 minutes. Then pour on ½ pint (300 ml) water, stirring, and add the sliced oranges and the cloves, bayleaf and seasoning.

Replace the meat in the pan, cover with the lid, and cook in a slow to moderate oven, 325°F (170°C) Gas Mark 3 (bottom right-hand oven in a 4-door Aga) for about 3 hours. Remove from the oven, and leave overnight, skim off any fat which has collected on the surface, and reheat for 1 hour at the same temperature before you want to eat. Put the meat on a warm plate, and slice it, spooning some of the vegetables and juices from the casserole over each helping.

Mushroom, Cheese & Garlic Soufflé

Many people regard the making of soufflés with awe. They are, quite wrongly, under the impression that soufflés require a lot of skill in their production, and that you have to be some sort of culinary genius to concoct one. I felt just the same about them until I plucked up courage one day and, following a recipe word for word, made a stunning cheese soufflé. Flushed with my success I started experimenting and now when I can't think what to make for supper I opt for a soufflé.

The only thing to remember about soufflés is that they have to be eaten straight from the oven – they just won't wait for anyone, as they quickly lose their glorious, puffy height. So we usually only eat them in the winter months when I can be sure that Godfrey will be home for dinner at the pre-arranged time. In the months when the hotel is operating, there are many unforeseen hitches which tend to crop up just as he is leaving to come home for supper, and sunken soufflé is a sorry sight indeed.

A soufflé is a marvellous last-minute dish for when unexpected visitors arrive. You can nearly always be sure of having an onion, some garlic, a bit of cheese and, of course, eggs in the house. And this is all you need to make a soufflé. Or add some finely chopped mushrooms, like this:

3 oz (75 g) butter
1 onion, peeled and finely
  chopped
1 clove of garlic, peeled and
  finely chopped
4 oz (125 g) mushrooms,
  finely chopped
3 oz (75 g) plain flour
¾ pint (425 ml) milk
6 large eggs

salt and freshly ground black
  pepper
a pinch of ground nutmeg
4 oz (125 g) mature
  Lancashire or Cheddar
  cheese, grated
extra butter for greasing
grated Parmesan cheese,
  optional

Butter a soufflé dish, about 7 in (18 cm) in diameter, and dust with Parmesan cheese if you have some.

Melt the 3 oz (75 g) butter in a saucepan, add the chopped onion and garlic and cook gently for 7–10 minutes until the onion is soft and transparent. Add the finely chopped mushrooms, and cook for about 1 minute, then stir in the flour. Gradually add the milk, stirring all the time until the sauce boils. Take the saucepan off the heat and leave to cool. Then separate the eggs, putting the whites in a clean bowl and beating the yolks one by one into the cooled sauce. Season with salt, pepper and nutmeg and beat in the grated cheese. You can prepare the soufflé to this stage in the morning, ready for supper that evening if you wish.

About three quarters of an hour before you want to eat, whisk the egg whites until they are stiff, and, using a metal spoon, fold them quickly and thoroughly into the sauce. Pour this into the prepared soufflé dish, and bake in a hot oven, 425°F (220°C) Gas Mark 7 (the top right-hand oven in a 4-door Aga). Bake for 40 minutes; if the diners are not quite ready another 5–10 minutes in the oven won't hurt.

Serve immediately – the soufflé will be soft in the centre. Serve with a green or tomato salad, and with warm brown bread or rolls.

Pigeon & Steak Pie

Pigeons are wonderful birds to cook and eat. Not only are they delicious, but they need no plucking; if you slit the skin through the feather, the skin, feathers and all, just peels off, and you can then cut the breasts away from the rest of the bird. Because we somehow never get enough pigeons to make a dish on their own, I usually end up making a pie by adding some rump steak, which goes well with the pigeon meat. (What we call rump in Skye is not a grilling steak; it is a lean braising steak usually sold as topside or silverside in other parts of Britain.)

Serves 8

---

4 tablespoons sunflower seed oil

4 pigeons, with the breasts removed

2 lb (900 g) lean braising steak, cut in pieces about 2 in (5 cm) across

2 rashers of bacon, rinded and cut in pieces

2 onions, peeled and thinly sliced

8 oz (225 g) mushrooms, sliced

1 rounded tablespoon plain flour

½ pint (300 ml) stock

½ pint (300 ml) red wine

1 tablespoon redcurrant jelly

salt and freshly ground black pepper

12 oz (350 g) puff or flaky pastry

milk for glazing

Heat the oil in a saucepan and brown the pigeon breasts and the pieces of steak well on all sides. Remove from the pan and keep warm. Add the pieces of bacon and fry until brown, then remove them to the dish containing the pigeon and beef. Lower the heat under the saucepan and add the sliced onions to the pan; cook gently, stirring occasionally, for 10 minutes until the onions are soft and

47

transparent. Then put the sliced mushrooms in with the onions, cook for 1–2 minutes and stir in the flour. Gradually add the stock and red wine, stirring until the sauce boils; when it has boiled stir in the redcurrant jelly and the seasoning.

Put the meat, pigeon breasts and the sauce in a 3½ pint (2 litre) pie dish, and leave to cool. Cover with the pastry, decorate and brush the pie with milk. Bake in a hot oven 400°F (200°C) Gas Mark 6 (top right-hand oven in a 4-door Aga) for 20 minutes. Then lower the heat to 350°F (180°C) Gas Mark 4 (bottom right-hand oven in the Aga) and cook for a further 30 minutes until the pastry is golden brown.

Artichokes as a Vegetable

Jerusalem artichokes are good mashed and beaten together with potatoes or carrots as an accompaniment to a main course. If you are doing artichokes and potatoes, boil them together until both are cooked, drain well, mash until both are smooth. Then, using a wooden spoon, beat with some butter until you have a smooth purée. Beat in a little milk and, depending on quantities, 1 or 2 egg yolks. Season with salt and freshly ground black pepper and pile into a well-buttered ovenproof dish. You can prepare these mixed root vegetable purées in the morning and reheat them for dinner that night. If you are mixing carrots with either potatoes, artichokes or parsnips give the carrots more cooking time than the other vegetables.

Parsnips

Parsnips inspire the same extremes in people's tastes as artichokes; I find, that is, they either love them or loathe them. I love them, and luckily so do Godfrey and our girls.

Hugo will like them too when he is a bit older, because he already has them mashed up in his lunch from time to time – I am determined that he will like them.

Roast parsnips, roasted round a joint of lamb or beef, complement the meat well. It may sound strange, but parsnips also go well with fish.

Parsnip & Carrot Ragout

Parsnips mix well with carrots, and with some onion you can make this useful vegetable dish. It can be prepared ahead and left to cook slowly, thus cutting down on the last-minute rush for a dinner party.

Serves 6

4 medium-sized carrots	1 onion, peeled and finely sliced
4 fairly large parsnips	1 clove of garlic, peeled and finely chopped
2 oz (50 g) butter	$\frac{1}{4}$ pint (150 ml) chicken stock
	salt and freshly ground black pepper

Peel the carrots and parsnips, and cut both into fine strips. Melt the butter in a flameproof casserole, and add the finely sliced onion. Cook over a gentle heat until the onion is soft. Add the chopped garlic and the strips of carrot and parsnip. Cook for 2–3 minutes, stirring from time to time, until the vegetables are well coated with butter, then pour on the stock. Add some salt and freshly ground black pepper, and cover with a tightly fitting lid. Simmer very gently for about 45 minutes, or until the vegetables are really soft.

49

Crunchy Tops for Vegetables

All vegetable purées benefit from a crunchy top. For a contrast in textures sprinkle one of the following on top of any mashed or puréed concoction of vegetables:

Plain salted potato crisps, crushed and sprinkled thickly over the surface of the vegetables. (This is popular with children.)
Crisply cooked bacon, broken into small bits, and sprinkled over the surface either alone, or mixed with wholemeal breadcrumbs.
Nuts, fried in butter with some salt added, then strewn over the surface.

Carrot Cake

This recipe is one of my most precious. When we make it at Kinloch we call it Kinloch Gâteau. Some of our visitors regularly ask that it should feature on the menu the night they are dining with us. I wonder if anyone would choose it if we called it by its real name. The recipe was given to me by Caroline Wood, who came to help out at Ostaig for a few weeks in 1976, during a Clan Gathering. I have never met anyone who hasn't loved it, and when Isabella was 7 she requested it for her birthday cake.

This cake is best made the day before you want it and the cake without the filling freezes beautifully for weeks. With the filling and icing, don't freeze for much more than two or three weeks. It is quite a gooey sort of cake, and well suited to be a pudding for a party.

Serves 8–9

---

6 oz (175 g) plain flour, sieved
¾ rounded teaspoon baking powder
¾ rounded teaspoon bicarbonate of soda
¾ rounded teaspoon ground cinnamon
¼ rounded teaspoon salt
just less than ½ pint (300 ml) sunflower seed oil

12 oz (350 g) caster sugar
3 large eggs
8 oz (225 g) grated raw carrot
oil for greasing
For the filling and icing:
6 oz (175 g) cream cheese
6 oz (175 g) butter
8 oz (225 g) icing sugar
½ teaspoon vanilla essence

Sieve the dry ingredients together. Put the oil in a large bowl, add the sugar and, using an electric hand whisk, beat together. Add the eggs, one by one, beating well in between each one. Fold in the sieved dry ingredients, and lastly stir in the grated carrot.

Lightly grease a 10 in (25 cm) round cake tin and line it with siliconised paper, or grease the tin well and shake flour around the greased surface thoroughly. Spoon the mixture into the tin, bake in a moderate oven 350°F (180°C) Gas Mark 4 (middle shelf of the bottom right-hand oven in a 4-door Aga) for 45 minutes then lower the heat to 325°F (170°C) Gas Mark 3 (or move the tin to the bottom of the Aga oven) and bake for a further 20 minutes. Test by pushing a knife into the centre of the cake; if it comes out clean the cake is cooked. If the knife has a trace

51

of cake mixture sticking to its blade, put the cake back and test again after a further 15 minutes. When cooked, remove the cake from the oven, cool for 5 minutes in the tin, then turn out on to a cooling rack. Carefully peel off the paper, and leave to get completely cold.

When cold, make the filling. Beat together the cream cheese and butter and gradually add the icing sugar, sieving it as you add it. Beat together really well, adding the vanilla essence. Split the cake in half and fill and cover with the butter cream.

Pear & Ginger Mousse

Pears and ginger go well together.

Serves 8

---

1 level tablespoon gelatine
4 large eggs, separated
4 oz (125 g) caster sugar
2 tablespoons ginger syrup
½ pint (300 ml) double cream, whipped but not too stiffly
6 pieces of preserved ginger, drained from their syrup

and cut in fine slivers
8 pears, peeled, cored and cut into quarters
extra whipped cream and ginger to decorate, optional, or toasted flaked almonds

---

Put 3 tablespoons cold water in a small saucepan and sprinkle in the gelatine. Leave to soak a little then warm over gentle heat until the gelatine is dissolved. Leave to cool. Beat the egg yolks, gradually adding the caster sugar, until the mixture is thick and pale. Beat in the ginger syrup. Stir in the dissolved gelatine, mixing thoroughly, then fold in the whipped cream.

Fold in the fine slivers of ginger, and leave until the

mixture is beginning to set. Then quickly whisk the egg whites until stiff, and fold them into the creamy ginger mixture. Lay the prepared pear quarters in the bottom of a shallow dish, and cover with the ginger mousse. Decorate if you like with more whipped cream and bits of ginger, or with toasted flaked almonds sprinkled over the surface.

Apple Pie

Some people make a shallow apple pie with pastry top and bottom. I prefer to make a deeper pie with more apples, and pastry only on the top. I also like lots of spices, grated orange rind and raisins in my apple pie. All these items are optional – just leave out what you don't like.

Serves 8–10

For the pastry:
4 oz (125 g) butter, chilled
6 oz (175 g) plain flour
1 oz (25 g) icing sugar
milk for glazing
For the apple filling:
8 cooking apples, peeled and cored
lemon juice
1 rounded tablespoon plain flour
8 rounded tablespoons demerara or soft brown sugar

2 rounded teaspoons ground cinnamon
½ rounded teaspoon ground cloves, or 6 whole cloves
1 rounded teaspoon grated nutmeg
grated rind and juice of 2 oranges
2 rounded tablespoons raisins

Blend the pastry ingredients together with 2 tablespoons cold water in a food processor, or mixer using the dough hook, until just formed into a dough. Wrap the dough in

53

cling film and put in the refrigerator until you are ready to roll out.

Slice the apples thinly into a 3 pint (1.7 litre) pie dish and sprinkle with lemon juice to prevent browning. Mix together the flour, sugar, spices and orange rind, and mix them thoroughly into the sliced apples, together with the raisins. Measure the orange juice and make up to ½ pint (300 ml) with water and pour over the apples. Then roll out the pastry and cover the top of the pie. Slash the pastry surface in 2–3 places, to let the steam out as the pie cooks.

Brush the pastry with milk, and cook in a hot oven 400°F (200°C) Gas Mark 6 (or top right-hand oven in a 4-door Aga) for 20 minutes, then lower the heat to moderate, 350°F (180°C) Gas Mark 4 (bottom right-hand oven in a 4-door Aga) and cook until the pastry is golden brown. Serve with either whipped cream, or best of all, vanilla ice cream.

March

March is too early for new lamb or spring vegetables, and too early by far for summery fruits. In fact, it is a bleak month for inspiration from the green-grocers' shops. Yet gastronomically I find I need cheering up in March, because here in Skye spring seems to be on a work-to-rule, and not much progress is apparent. The trees don't appear any less bare, and nothing much comes up in the garden. It's always a treat to find the first few primroses, which grow here in profusion in the roadside verges and in the bleakest rock faces.

March also brings the one aspect of spring I hate, that is spring cleaning. Being blessed with appalling short-sight, I find that by removing my specs my conscience is easier, for I can barely see dust, and certainly not cobwebs. But alas, one cannot expect people to stay in hotels which aren't clean, so Kinloch is given a thorough cleaning in spring.

But March does bring a source of great inspiration in the form of Shrove Tuesday. Depending on the date of Easter this festival generally falls in March, and traditionally pancakes are eaten on that day. On Shrove Tuesday we eat them with lemon juice and caster sugar, but pancakes are so versatile, and can make such delicious savoury and sweet dishes that they reappear throughout the month. They freeze well, providing they are going to be eaten hot. (If they are frozen, thawed, and eaten cold they tend to be rather leathery.)

The basic pancake batter is simple and quick to make, and can have various additions to it. A couple of table-spoons of finely chopped herbs not only enhances the appearance of savoury pancakes (especially if they are to be filled with a pale-coloured filling) but gives them a lovely fresh flavour. For a sweet pancake dish, the pancake batter can have 1 oz (25g) cocoa substituted for 1 oz (25 g) of the flour in the basic pancake batter. Making pancakes is a lengthy process, but worth every minute.

First Courses

Basic Pancake Recipe
Stilton-stuffed Pancakes with Tomato Sauce
Spinach, Turmeric and Lemon Soup
Mussels with Garlic, Parsley and White Wine

Main Courses

Eggs with Onion and Cheese Sauce
Pancakes Stuffed with Chicken and Mushrooms
Chicken Pizzaiola
Spinach Roulade with Kidneys, Bacon and Mushrooms
Scallops with White Wine and Cheese Sauce
Mushroom and Onion Cream Tart

Vegetables

Frozen Sliced Beans with Fried Salted Almonds

Desserts

My Version of Crêpes Suzette
Chocolate Pancakes
Hot Plum and Orange Compôte
Plum and Port Mousse
Cinnamon Biscuits

Basic Pancake Recipe

Makes 16

---

4 oz (125 g) plain flour
2 eggs
¼ pint (150 ml) milk

3 tablespoons melted butter,
or sunflower seed oil
¼ rounded teaspoon salt
butter for frying

Work the ingredients in a blender until they are smooth, and leave the mixture for 1–2 hours before you make up the pancakes.

When you are ready to start making them, drop a piece of butter, a small teaspoonful, into a 7 in (18 cm) frying pan. (Do not be tempted to substitute margarine, the pancakes will stick to the pan.) Melt the butter, swirling it around in the pan until it is well greased all over. Take a large tablespoon of the pancake batter and pour it into the pan, tilting the pan to cover the surface with a thin layer of batter. Cook on a moderate heat, until the bottom of the pancake is golden brown, then I find that the easiest way to turn the pancake over to cook on the other side is to carefully use my fingers. When the pancake is cooked on both sides, slip it on to a cooling rack, and keep warm, or let cool, depending on what you intend to do with it.

Stilton-stuffed Pancakes with Tomato Sauce

This recipe is one of our favourite first courses. It is best made with fresh basil, but as I can't often get hold of fresh, I usually have to make do with dried. The sauce freezes well and can be used for numerous other recipes; it is excellent as a sauce with pasta.

2 egg whites
12 oz (350 g) Stilton cheese
freshly ground black pepper
16 pancakes, see above, with
    2 rounded tablespoons
    finely chopped herbs added
    to the basic batter
4 tablespoons olive oil
2 medium-sized onions,
    peeled and chopped
1 carrot, peeled and chopped
1 stick celery, sliced

2 cloves of garlic, peeled and
    finely chopped
2 × 14 oz (398 g) tins
    tomatoes
salt and freshly ground black
    pepper
½ rounded teaspoon sugar
½ rounded teaspoon dried
    basil or ½ tablespoon
    chopped fresh

Whisk the egg whites until frothy. Crumble the Stilton and mix with the whites to a firm paste. Season with the black pepper. Butter a shallow ovenproof dish. Divide the Stilton mixture between the pancakes, roll each pancake up, and tuck the ends of the rolled pancake under, to form a sort of parcel shape. This is to prevent any of the Stilton stuffing from oozing out as they cook. Lay the pancake parcels neatly in the buttered dish. Bake in a hot oven, 400°F (200°C) Gas Mark 6 (top right-hand oven in a 4-door Aga) for 15 minutes.

To make the sauce, heat the oil in a saucepan. Add the chopped and sliced vegetables, and cook over a gentle heat for 10–15 minutes, until the onion is soft and transparent. Add the contents of the tins of tomatoes, and the seasonings. With the lid half on the saucepan, simmer the sauce gently for 45 minutes – 1 hour. Remove from the heat, cool, purée in a blender and sieve. This gives a good, well-flavoured, smooth sauce. Serve separately, in a jug or sauceboat, with the Stilton-stuffed pancakes.

Spinach, Turmeric & Lemon Soup

Serves 6–8

2 oz (50 g) butter
2 medium-sized onions,
   peeled and chopped
2 lb (900 g) frozen spinach,
   thawed
rind of 1 lemon, pared off
   with a potato peeler
juice of 1 lemon

1 rounded tablespoon
   turmeric
2 pints (1.1 litres) chicken
   stock
salt and freshly ground black
   pepper
8 dessertspoons single cream,
   or natural yogurt

Melt the butter in a saucepan and add the chopped onion. Cook over a gentle heat for 10 minutes or so, until the onions are soft and transparent, then add the thawed spinach. Put in the lemon rind, juice, turmeric, chicken stock and seasoning. Bring just to the boil and simmer very gently, for 30 minutes. Remove from the heat, cool, and purée in a blender. Reheat and serve with a spoonful of cream or natural yogurt in the middle of each plateful of soup. Serve with warm garlic buttered rolls.

Mussels with Garlic, Parsley & White Wine

We are so lucky to live where we do – not just in Skye, but right on the sea. There is a beach at the bottom of our garden, and the rocks are covered with mussels. We have phases of mussel-eating which, come to think of it, go with the fine weather. There is no fun in picking a bucketful of mussels from the rocks in the pouring rain, but in fine and sunny weather it is a lovely pastime. As the sea is totally unpolluted here, it is perfectly safe to eat the mussels.

60

4 pints (about 2 kg medium-
sized mussels
1½ pints (850 ml) water and
white wine mixed

2 cloves of garlic, peeled and
finely chopped
4 tablespoons finely chopped
parsley
freshly ground black pepper

Scrub each mussel thoroughly under running cold water, discarding any that are open. This takes time but there is no short cut and if not washed thoroughly they will be gritty. Put the mussels in a large saucepan, pour on the mixed water and wine, and add to the pan the finely chopped garlic, parsley and plenty of pepper (nature provides enough salt). Cover with a tightly fitting lid, and cook over a moderate heat, for about 10 minutes, stirring the mussels once or twice during cooking, to mix up the ones on the bottom with those on the top.

Serve in large soup plates, with plates for the empty shells, and plenty of brown bread to mop up the juices. Discard any unopened shells.

Eggs with Onion & Cheese Sauce

This is one of those lovely supper or lunch dishes that can be prepared ahead and heated through in the oven at the last minute. As with all egg dishes, it is very filling. Lancashire cheese is one of the best cheeses for cooking with.

Serves 6 as a main course. If you are making this for a first course, 8 eggs would be enough

---

12 eggs	*8 oz (225 g) Lancashire*
3 oz (75 g) butter	*cheese, grated*
2 large onions, peeled and	*a little salt and lots of*
very thinly sliced	*freshly ground black*
3 oz (75 g) plain flour	*pepper*
1½ pints (850 ml) milk	*butter for greasing*

Hard-boil the eggs and butter a shallow ovenproof dish. Melt the 3 oz (75 g) butter in a saucepan, add the sliced onions and cook, gently, for about 10 minutes, until the onions are soft and transparent. Don't let them turn colour.

Stir in the flour, and cook for 1–2 minutes, then gradually add the milk, stirring all the time until the sauce boils. Take the saucepan off the heat and stir in most of the grated cheese, reserving some for sprinkling on top of the finished dish. Season.

Shell the hard-boiled eggs, slice them and arrange in an even layer over the bottom of the buttered dish. Pour the cheese and onion sauce over them, and sprinkle with the remaining grated cheese. Put the dish in a moderate oven, 350°F (180°C) Gas Mark 4 (bottom right-hand oven in a 4-door Aga) for 15 minutes, or until the cheese on the top is melted and the sauce is just bubbling gently.

Serve with salad and brown bread.

Pancakes Stuffed with Chicken & Mushrooms

Pancakes can be a marvellous way to dress up left-over meat or fish. There is a certain panache attached to a dish composed of pancakes (especially if they are referred to as *crêpes!*) and a small quantity of left-over chicken, for example, can be padded out with a good, tasty sauce.

Serves 8

---

3 oz (75 g) butter
1 medium-sized onion, peeled and very finely chopped
8 oz (250 g) mushrooms, sliced
3 oz (75 g) flour
1½ pints (850 ml) milk
2 tablespoons sherry

4 oz (125 g) cooked chicken, diced fairly small (or use left-over ham or salmon)
salt and freshly ground black pepper
a pinch of ground nutmeg
16 pancakes, see page 58
2 oz (50 g) grated cheese

Melt the butter in a saucepan, add the finely chopped onion and cook over a gentle heat, stirring from time to time, until the onion is soft, but not turning colour. Add the sliced mushrooms to the pan, cook for a further 2 minutes, then stir in the flour. Gradually stir in the milk, stirring all the time until the sauce comes to the boil. Take the pan off the heat and stir in the sherry and seasoning. Leave the sauce to cool completely before adding the chicken.

Butter a shallow ovenproof dish. Divide the cold sauce between the pancakes, roll them up and lay in rows in the dish. Sprinkle the grated cheese over, and bake in a moderately hot oven, 375°F (190°C) Gas Mark 5 (bottom right-hand oven in a 4-door Aga) for 40 minutes.

You can get the dish ready to bake in the morning, so all you need to do in the evening is pop it in the oven. Serve with warm brown rolls and a green salad.

Chicken Pizzaiola

This recipe is ideal for those who are counting calories.

Serves 6

4½ lb (2 kg) chicken or 6
  chicken joints or fillets
4 tablespoons olive oil
2 large onions, peeled and
  thinly sliced
1 or 2 cloves of garlic, peeled
  and finely chopped

2 × 15 oz (425 g) tins
  tomatoes
salt and freshly ground black
  pepper
½ rounded teaspoon sugar
½ rounded teaspoon dried
  basil

Heat the oil in a large frying pan or flameproof casserole.
Brown the chicken, pieces or whole, really well on all sides.
Remove and keep warm.

Lower the heat under the pan, and add the thinly sliced
onions and the finely chopped garlic and cook gently,
stirring from time to time, until the onions are soft and
transparent. Add the tomatoes, salt and pepper, sugar and
basil and stir until boiling, breaking up the tomatoes as
much as you can with the wooden spoon.

Replace the chicken in the sauce. If you are using fillets
of chicken, simmer in the sauce for 15 minutes or so, until
when you stab them with the point of a knife the juices that
run are clear. If you are using chicken joints on the bone
they will need to simmer for 30–40 minutes, turning them
over once during cooking. If you are using a whole chicken,
cover the casserole with a lid and cook in a moderate oven,
350°F (180°C) Gas Mark 4 (bottom right-hand oven in a
4-door Aga) for 1–1¼ hours. Again, stab the chicken in the
thigh (sounds so painful) with the point of a knife, and the
chicken is cooked when the juices run clear.

Put chicken fillets or pieces in a serving dish and pour the
tomato sauce over them. If you are using a whole chicken,

carve it, put the slices in a serving dish, before pouring the sauce over.

This is good served with noodles, preferably green ones. Cook the noodles in boiling salted water until just tender, but not soft, drain well and stir in ¼ pint (150 ml) single cream before serving.

Spinach Roulade with Kidneys, Bacon & Mushrooms

This amount serves 6 people for a main course. You can make it for a first course, leaving out the kidneys and bacon, in which case it will serve 8.

---

2 lb (900 g) frozen spinach, thawed	*4 lambs' kidneys, skinned and cored*
4 eggs, separated	*8 oz (225 g) mushrooms, sliced*
4 oz (125 g) butter	
salt and freshly ground black pepper	*2 rounded tablespoons plain flour*
grated nutmeg	*about ½ pint (300 ml) milk*
6 rashers bacon, preferably smoked	

Line a Swiss roll tin measuring about 10 × 12 in (25 × 30 cm) with a piece of siliconised paper. Squeeze as much water as possible from the thawed spinach, and whizz in a food processor, adding the egg yolks one by one, and 1 oz (25 g) butter, salt, black pepper and ¼ rounded teaspoon nutmeg. If you don't have a food processor, purée the spinach a little at a time in a blender, gradually adding the egg yolks, butter and seasoning.

Whisk the whites in a separate bowl, and fold them into the spinach and yolk purée. Pour into the lined tin, smoothing it evenly. Bake in a moderate oven, 350°F (180°C) Gas Mark 4 (bottom right-hand oven in a 4-door Aga) for 20–25 minutes, until firm to the touch.

While the spinach is cooking, make the sauce. Grill or fry the bacon until the rashers are crisp. Put them to drain on a piece of kitchen paper. Cut each kidney into about 8 pieces, add to the bacon fat and cook for 1–2 minutes (beware – an over-cooked kidney can become tough). Put the pieces of kidney on one side to keep warm, along with the crisp bacon rashers.

Melt the remaining butter in a saucepan, and add the mushrooms. Cook for 2 minutes, then stir in the flour. Cook for a further minute, then gradually add the milk, stirring all the time. The sauce should not be too runny. Stir until the sauce comes to the boil and season with salt and pepper and a pinch of nutmeg. Break up the crisp bacon rashers into fairly small pieces and stir these and the cooked kidney into the mushroom sauce.

When the roulade mixture is cooked remove it from the oven. Put a fresh piece of siliconised paper on a work surface and tip the cooked mixture on to it. Carefully peel the old paper off the back. Spread the bacon, kidney and mushroom sauce over the spinach roulade, and roll up from the long side, like a long Swiss roll. Slide it on to a serving dish, and serve hot with baked potatoes and a green salad.

Scallops with White Wine & Cheese Sauce

Serves 6

---

about 30 medium-sized
    shelled whole scallops, or
    18 large scallops, halved
1 pint (570 ml) milk
1 small onion, peeled and cut
    in half
blade of mace
freshly ground black pepper

2 oz (50 g) butter
1 level teaspoon curry powder
2 rounded tablespoons plain
    flour
1 sherry glass of white wine
3 oz (75 g) cheese,
    preferably Lancashire but
    Cheddar will do, grated

Put the scallops in a saucepan and cover with the milk and ½ pint (300 ml) water. Add to the pan the onion, mace and black pepper, and put the saucepan over a gentle heat. Bring the liquid slowly to simmering point, then draw the pan off the heat and leave the scallops to cool in the liquid for about 20 minutes.

Then melt the butter in another saucepan, stir in the curry powder and flour, and cook for 2 minutes. Strain the liquid off the cooled scallops, and gradually stir it into the flour and butter mixture, stirring until the sauce boils. Stir in the white wine, then draw the pan off the heat and add the grated cheese, stirring until it is all melted. Put the scallops into the sauce and pour into an ovenproof dish to keep warm until needed – it won't keep hot satisfactorily for much more than 20 minutes. Serve with boiled rice, brown if possible, and beans with fried, sliced almonds stirred through them.

Mushroom & Onion Cream Tart

This is a lovely filling for a tart. Cream tarts can be horribly stodgy, so to achieve the soft and creamy set to the custard, use mostly egg yolks. If you use whole eggs the whites tend to give the custard a rubbery texture.

Serves 6 as a main course, 8 as a first course

4 oz (125 g) butter, chilled and cut into pieces
5 oz (150 g) plain flour
1 rounded tablespoon icing sugar
½ teaspoon salt
For the filling:
3 tablespoons sunflower seed oil
4 large onions, peeled and sliced as thinly as possible
1 or 2 cloves of garlic, peeled and finely chopped
8 oz (225 g) mushrooms, sliced
salt and freshly ground black pepper
1 egg
3 egg yolks
¾ pint (425 ml) creamy milk
finely chopped parsley, optional

Put the butter, flour, icing sugar and salt in a food processor and whizz until the mixture is like breadcrumbs. Pat it gently into an 8–9 in (20–23 cm) flan dish and prick the base with a fork. Put in the refrigerator for 30 minutes. Bake blind in a moderate oven, 350°F (180°C) Gas Mark 4 (bottom right-hand oven in a 4-door Aga) for 20 minutes.

Heat the oil in a saucepan and add the onions. Cook gently, with the pan partially covered with its lid, for 20 minutes, stirring the onions from time to time. The onions will then be really softened.

Add the chopped garlic to the pan, together with the sliced mushrooms, and cook for a further 2–3 minutes. Season with a little salt and lots of freshly ground black pepper. Beat together the egg, yolks and milk and pour into the onion and mushroom mixture. Mix well. Pour into the cooked pastry case and bake in a moderate oven, 350°F (180°C) Gas Mark 4 (bottom right-hand oven in a 4-door Aga) for 20–30 minutes, or until the custard filling is just firm to the touch. It will go on cooking for a few minutes after you have taken it out of the oven, so don't leave it until the custard is set too firmly.

If you like, sprinkle finely chopped parsley over the surface of the tart before serving it.

Frozen Sliced Beans with Fried Salted Almonds

I much prefer fresh vegetables, but there comes a time especially living in Skye, when there isn't much variety to choose from. So inevitably during the spring months I find myself reaching for frozen beans. I have to confess that I love them anyway, but with the addition of a few sliced almonds, fried in butter with salt to provide a good contrasting crunch, they are delicious.

Serves 4

---

1 lb (500 g) frozen sliced beans
pinch of bicarbonate of soda
1 oz (25 g) butter

½ rounded teaspoon salt
2 oz (50 g) sliced almonds

Bring some water to the boil in a saucepan, put in a pinch of bicarbonate of soda (which keeps the bright, fresh colour of the beans) and put in the frozen beans. Bring the water back to the boil, and boil for 2 minutes, then drain well.

In a saucepan, melt the butter, add to it the salt, and the sliced almonds. Fry, shaking the pan from time to time, until the almonds are golden brown. Stir the fried almonds into the drained, cooked beans, and put into a warmed serving dish.

My Version of Crêpes Suzette

Serves 8

For the pancakes:
4 oz (125 g) plain flour
2 eggs
¼ pint (150 ml) milk
3 tablespoons melted butter
   or sunflower seed oil
grated rind of 1 orange
1 oz (25 g) caster sugar
butter for frying
For the filling:
4 oz (125 g) butter

4 oz (125 g) icing sugar,
   sieved
grated rind of 1 orange
4 tablespoons brandy or an
   orange liqueur, such as
   cointreau
To finish:
butter for greasing
1–2 rounded tablespoons
   icing sugar, sieved
3 tablespoons brandy

Whizz the pancake ingredients together with ½ pint (300 ml) water in a blender until really well mixed and leave for an hour or two before making up. Cook as for the Basic Pancake Recipe (page 58), making 16 pancakes.

For the filling, cream together the butter and sieved icing sugar. Beat in the grated orange rind, and then beat in the brandy or orange liqueur very gradually, almost a teaspoon at a time.

Divide the orange flavoured butter cream between the pancakes, and spread it evenly over them. Fold each pancake in half, then in half again, so you have triangles. Butter a shallow ovenproof dish. Lay the triangular pancakes in rows, slightly overlapping each other. If you want to freeze the dish, at this point cover with cling film and put into the freezer. When ready to cook, take them out and thaw them and finish as if they were freshly made.

To finish, put the dish into a moderately hot oven, 375°F (190°C) Gas Mark 5 (top right-hand oven in a 4-door Aga) for 20 minutes, or until the buttery filling in the pancakes has completely melted. Take out of the oven and dust with sieved icing sugar. Warm the brandy and set fire to it while still in the pan, then pour it over the heated pancakes. Blow the flames out before they char the pancakes. Serve warm, with whipped cream.

Chocolate Pancakes

Serves 8

For the pancakes:
3 oz (75 g) plain flour
1 oz (25 g) cocoa powder
2 eggs
1 oz (25 g) caster sugar
¼ pint (150 ml) milk
3 tablespoons melted butter or sunflower seed oil
butter for frying and greasing

2 rounded tablespoons icing sugar, sieved
For the chestnut filling:
2 × 15 oz (425 g) tins sweetened chestnut purée
a few drops of vanilla essence
½ pint (300 ml) double cream, whipped

Work together the flour, cocoa powder, eggs, caster sugar, milk and melted butter with ½ pint (300 ml) water in a blender until well mixed. Leave for an hour or two before making the pancakes. Cook as for the Basic Pancake Recipe (page 58), making 16 pancakes.

Tinned chestnut purée tends to be rather solid when it emerges from its tin. If you have a food processor put the purée into the processor, and whizz around to make it smooth and softer, so that it will blend more easily with the whipped cream. If you have no food processor, put the purée into a bowl, and break down with a wooden spoon until it is as smooth as you can manage.

Fold together the chestnut purée, vanilla essence and the whipped cream. Divide evenly between the pancakes, roll them up and lay in neat rows in a buttered ovenproof, shallow dish. Dust quite liberally with sieved icing sugar. Shortly before serving them, heat the grill, and put the dish of pancakes under for just enough time to caramelise the icing sugar – only 1–2 minutes and keep watching all the time.

Serve the pancakes with a good chocolate sauce.

Chocolate Sauce

This sauce can be made ahead of serving and kept for days in a screw-topped jar in the refrigerator. Heat it up before serving. The cup I use for measuring holds 7 fl oz (200 ml).

---

1 cup of sugar	*3 level tablespoons cocoa*
1 cup of boiling water	*powder*
1 teaspoon vanilla essence	*3 oz (75 g) butter*
	3 tablespoons golden syrup

Put all the ingredients together in a saucepan. Bring to the boil and simmer gently for 4–5 minutes.

Hot Plum & Orange Compôte

Serves 6

1½ lb (700 g) plums	*sugar to taste*
6 oranges	

Cut each plum in half, removing the stone. Cut each half

72

into half again and put them in an ovenproof dish.

Using a serrated knife, cut the skin and as much of the pith as possible off each orange. Working over the dish to catch the juice, cut in between the membranes towards the centre of each orange to give segments. Put these into the dish with the quartered plums and add the juice. Sprinkle over the sugar, about 2 tablespoons to start with, you can always add more. Cover the dish with a piece of foil, and bake in a moderate oven, 350°F (180°C) Gas Mark 4 (bottom right-hand oven in a 4-door Aga) for 20 minutes. Taste, and if you think it needs more sugar, stir in another spoonful. Serve with Cinnamon Biscuits (page 75).

Plum & Port Mousse

Plums and port seem to go together well. This is a most refreshing mousse, and nicely rounds off a rich dinner.

Serves 6–8

1 lb (500 g) plums	3 eggs, separated
4 rounded tablespoons granulated sugar	4 oz (125 g) caster sugar
2 sherry glasses port	1/4 pint (150 ml) double cream, whipped
1 level tablespoon gelatine	

Put the plums into a saucepan with the granulated sugar and cover with a lid. Put the pan over a low heat and as the plums begin to cook they will make juice. Cook until they begin to fall apart, then remove them from the heat, cool, and remove the stones, using a spoon and fork. Purée the stoned plums in a blender, together with the port. Sieve the purée to remove the skins and coarse fibres.

Put 4 tablespoons cold water in a small saucepan and sprinkle in the gelatine. Leave to soften, then heat very gently until the gelatine is completely dissolved. Leave the liquid to cool.

Beat the egg yolks, adding the caster sugar to them gradually until thick and very pale in colour. Fold in the cooled plum and port purée.

Whisk the egg whites until stiff. Stir the dissolved gelatine into the plum mixture, then fold in the whipped cream, and lastly fold in the stiffly whisked egg whites, using a metal spoon. Pour the mousse into a glass or china serving dish and chill until set.

Cinnamon Biscuits

Serves 6

4 oz (125 g) butter
2 oz (50 g) caster sugar
4 oz (125 g) self-raising
flour

1 rounded dessertspoon
ground cinnamon

Beat together the butter and sugar, and sieve in the flour and cinnamon gradually, beating until you have a stiff ball of dough. Take pieces about the size of a walnut, and roll into balls between the palms of your hands. Put them on a baking tray. Flatten each ball slightly, and press the back of a fork on top of each. Bake in a moderate oven, 350°F (180°C) Gas Mark 4 (bottom right-hand oven of a 4-door Aga) for 10–15 minutes or until golden brown. The biscuits will still be softish but will firm up on cooling. Leave them on the baking tray for 2–3 minutes, then transfer to a cooling rack. Serve with Hot Plum and Orange Compôte.

April

Lovely April brings with it the first real green growth on the trees and hedges. Primroses are thick in the banks along the road-sides and, usually, there is some good weather. April also generally brings Easter, which means the first busy time of the year at Kinloch. Although our small hotel is open all year round, I feel that the year starts properly, work-wise, with the Easter holidays.

Inspiration in the kitchen rides high at the start of the season, with lots of new ideas to be tried out. Eggs and chickens are synonymous with Easter, but delicious young rhubarb is also plentiful. Rhubarb is versatile, and luckily most people love it. Its flavour goes well with all sorts of others, but especially well with ginger, and with orange. When rhubarb is available, it is well worth while to make the most of it.

First Courses

Eggs Niçoise
Mushroom Soup
Bacon, Prawn and Cream Cheese Pâté
Mushroom and Sardine Pâté
Onion Soup with Toasted Cheese Croûtons

Main Courses

Fish Pie
Chicken and Broccoli in Mayonnaise Cream Sauce
Lamb Casseroled with Spices and Apricots
Smoked Haddock Roulade with Scallops
Sole Florentine

Desserts

Rhubarb Fudge Crumble
Rhubarb Meringue Pie
Rhubarb and Ginger Syllabub
Ginger Shortbread Fingers
Extremely Rich Chocolate and Ginger Pudding

Eggs Niçoise

This is a most popular first course at both Kinloch and Ardvasar hotels. It can also be a summer lunch dish, served with a tomato salad and brown bread or rolls. It can be made the day before it is required and kept, covered, in the refrigerator. You can adjust the amount of anchovy essence to suit your taste – we like rather a lot. Do not be tempted to add salt to the recipe, as both the anchovy essence and the chicken stock cube are quite salty, and will probably be enough for most palates.

Serves 6

1 chicken stock cube
1 level tablespoon gelatine
8 hard-boiled eggs, shelled and roughly chopped
8 tablespoons mayonnaise
¼ pint (150 ml) double cream, whipped

1 dessertspoon anchovy essence
freshly ground black pepper
2 oz (50 g) tin anchovy fillets, drained and cut lengthwise into strips
10 black olives, halved and stoned

Dissolve the chicken stock cube in ½ pint (300 ml) boiling water and sprinkle in the gelatine. Stir until there are no granules left and leave to cool. When quite cold and just beginning to set, stir in the chopped hard-boiled eggs.

Stir together the mayonnaise and the whipped cream. Add the anchovy essence and some black pepper, then fold in the egg mixture. Pour into a dish to set. When set, decorate the top with strips of anchovies arranged in a lattice design, and put half a black olive in each space. If you find anchovies too salty, drain them from the oil in their tin, and leave them to soak in a small dish of milk for a few hours. Pat dry before cutting into strips to decorate the finished eggs niçoise.

Mushroom Soup

In this recipe for mushroom soup you can add as much or as little cream as you like, or a spoonful of yoghurt on each helping is a pleasant change.

Serves 6

---

2 oz (50 g) butter
1 large onion, peeled and
    finely sliced
1 lb (500 g) mushrooms,
    thinly sliced
1 clove of garlic, peeled and
    finely chopped

1 heaped tablespoon
    wholemeal flour
2 pints (1.1 litres) good
    chicken stock
salt and freshly ground black
    pepper
pinch of grated nutmeg

Melt the butter in a saucepan, and add the sliced onion. Cook over a low to moderate heat until the onion is softened and transparent. Add the sliced mushrooms (don't peel the mushrooms as the flavour lies in the skin) and the garlic, and cook for a few more minutes, stirring. Then stir in the flour until it is well mixed with the mushrooms and onion. Stir in the chicken stock and the seasoning and simmer for about 20 minutes. Cool and purée in a blender. Taste to see if it needs more seasoning and reheat. Serve with warm brown rolls.

Bacon, Prawn & Cream Cheese Pâté

Bacon and shellfish go well together. This pâté is very quick and easy to make, and is heavenly to eat. We get huge, delicious prawns, up to 3 in (7.5 cm) long. Sometimes we get squat lobster tails, which are very good for this recipe.

Serves 6

---

3 oz (75 g) cooked, shelled prawns
3 rashers bacon
8 oz (250 g) cream cheese
1 clove of garlic, peeled and very finely chopped

freshly ground black pepper
1 tablespoon lemon juice
1 rounded tablespoon finely chopped parsley

Chop the prawns. Fry the bacon until crisp, drain on kitchen paper and break into small pieces. If you have a food processor, put the cream cheese in and whizz until smooth. Otherwise put the cream cheese into a bowl and pound it until it is as smooth as possible.

Don't add the rest of the ingredients to the food processor, because the whole pâté will become too smooth; one of its attractions is the different textures. So scoop the smooth cream cheese into a bowl, and add the rest of the ingredients, mixing them together well.

Heap into a serving dish and serve with brown bread or toast.

Mushroom & Sardine Pâté

This is a most unusual pâté. Don't be put off by the sardines; my husband loathes sardines, but loves this pâté. It doesn't freeze very well – it goes watery – but you can make it 3 or 4 days in advance and keep it in the refrigerator.

Serves 6–8

---

3 oz (75 g) butter
8 oz (250 g) mushrooms, sliced
2 × 4½ oz (140 g) tins sardines, drained of their oil

8 oz (250 g) cream cheese
2 tablespoons lemon juice
salt and freshly ground black pepper

Melt the butter in a frying pan and sauté the mushrooms. Mix with the rest of the ingredients in a food processor or blender and season with a little salt and a lot of freshly ground black pepper. Pile into a serving dish and chill. Serve with wholemeal toast.

Onion Soup with Toasted Cheese Croûtons

I love both onions and garlic, and both are extremely good for you. This soup is easy, and makes a very good first course, or it can make a substantial lunch dish.

Serves 4

4 large onions, peeled and halved

2 oz (50 g) butter

1 clove of garlic, peeled and finely chopped

14 oz (400 g) tin of consommé

1 wineglass white wine (just less than ¼ pint/150 ml)

salt and freshly ground black pepper

4 slices of bread, crusts trimmed off

4 oz (125 g) Lancashire cheese, grated

Slice the halved onions as thinly as possible. Melt the butter in a saucepan, and add the sliced onions and the garlic. Cook over a gentle heat for 10–15 minutes, until the onions are soft and transparent. Pour in the consommé and an equal quantity of water, the white wine and a little seasoning. Simmer gently for 30 minutes with the lid off the pan. Toast the bread and cut each slice into pieces about 1 in (2.5 cm) square.

When you are ready to serve, heat the grill until it is red hot. Ladle the hot soup into 4 soup plates, sprinkle toasted squares of bread on top and divide the grated cheese between them. Put each plate under the hot grill, to melt the cheese, and serve immediately – taking care not to burn yourself on the hot plates.

Fish Pie

So many people are put off fish pie for life by ghastly experiences during school days. It is, sadly, one of those dishes which can be positively vandalised by institution cooks, which is such a pity, because a good fish pie is not only delicious, but it is versatile. It is the sort of dish which can be dressed up or down. You can take the basic combination of white and smoked fish and add hard-boiled eggs and parsley, with a creamy mashed potato top for a family lunch; or you can add a few prawns, sliced mushrooms, and a dash of white wine, with a puffed pastry lid for a more elegant dish.

This is a more every-day type of fish pie, though with a puffed pastry finish. A substitute for potato or pastry is a thick layer of crushed, plain salted potato crisps; this is a great favourite with children. The chopped tomato and parsley in the sauce save the pie from looking too anaemic.

Serves 6–8

1½ lb (700 g) white fish, such as haddock	3 tomatoes, skinned, seeded and chopped
1 lb (500 g) smoked haddock	salt and freshly ground black pepper
2 pints (1.1 litres) milk	2 hard-boiled eggs, shelled and chopped
1 onion, peeled	2 rounded tablespoons finely chopped parsley
1 blade of mace	
3 oz (75 g) butter	12 oz (350 g) puff pastry
3 oz (75 g) plain flour	milk for glazing
2 oz (50 g) cheese, grated	

Put the fish, the milk, onion and mace together in a saucepan and, over a low heat, bring gently to the boil. Simmer for 2 minutes, then remove the pan from the heat, and cool for 20 minutes or so. Strain off and reserve the cooking liquid. Remove all skin and bones from the fish and flake the flesh.

Melt the butter in a saucepan and stir in the flour. Let it cook for 2 minutes, then gradually pour on the milk from the fish, stirring all the time until the sauce boils. Take it off the heat and stir in the grated cheese and the flaked, cooked fish. Stir in the chopped tomatoes, a little salt and pepper, the hard-boiled eggs and parsley, and pour into a 3½ pint (2 litre) pie dish.

Roll out the puff pastry and cover the pie. Stick the point of a sharp knife through the pastry in two or three places, to let the steam out while the pastry is cooking. Decorate the surface of the pie with leftover pastry cut into leaf shapes. Brush the pie with milk, and bake in a hot oven, 425°F (220°C) Gas Mark 7 (top right-hand oven in a 4-door Aga) for 15 minutes, then lower the heat to 375°F (190°C) Gas Mark 5 (bottom right-hand oven in the Aga) and cook for a further 30 minutes, until the pastry is puffed up.

Chicken & Broccoli in Mayonnaise Cream Sauce

The sauce for this dish has some rather unlikely sounding ingredients in it. Don't be put off, because it is a most useful recipe: it can be made several hours ahead and reheated when needed; it also has the vegetables in with the chicken and the sauce, making extras unnecessary. Although the ingredients sound odd, their combination is quite delicious, giving a lovely velvety textured, tasty sauce.

Serves 6

4 lb (1.8 kg) chicken
1 onion, peeled and quartered
1 carrot, peeled and cut in chunks
bouquet garni
salt
a few black peppercorns
2 lb (900 g) frozen broccoli
freshly ground black pepper
butter for greasing
2 oz (50 g) butter
2 oz (50 g) plain flour

1 rounded tablespoon curry powder
7 oz (200 g) tin evaporated milk
4 tablespoons mayonnaise, see page 128
2 tablespoons lemon juice
2 oz (50 g) Cheddar cheese, grated
4 rounded tablespoons breadcrumbs or 2 small packets potato crisps, crushed

Put the chicken in a large saucepan and cover with water. Add the onion, carrot, bouquet garni, salt and peppercorns. Bring to the boil, cover with a lid and simmer gently for 1 hour or until the juices run clear when the point of a knife is stuck into the thigh. Leave to cool in the stock.

Put the broccoli into a saucepan of boiling salted water, and boil until the stalks are just tender. Drain, and refresh under running cold water, which will bring back the green colour. Butter a wide, shallow 3 pint (1.7 litre) ovenproof

85

dish, and put the drained broccoli spears in it. When the chicken is cool enough to handle, remove it from the stock, take off the skin and strip the meat from the bones. Spread the chicken meat evenly over the broccoli.

Melt the butter in a saucepan and stir in the flour and curry powder. Cook over a gentle heat for 1–2 minutes, then gradually stir in 1 pint (600 ml) of the stock in which the chicken cooked. Stir until the sauce boils. Remove from the heat and add the evaporated milk, mayonnaise, lemon juice and the grated cheese, stirring until the cheese has melted. Check the seasoning, and add some salt and pepper if needed. Pour the sauce over the chicken in the dish and sprinkle either breadcrumbs or crushed potato crisps over the surface.

Bake in a moderately hot oven, 375°F (190°C) Gas Mark 5 (bottom right-hand oven in a 4-door Aga) for 30 minutes or until the sauce is just bubbling.

Lamb Casseroled with Spices & Apricots

This is a lovely recipe, and I usually serve it with boiled brown rice.

Serves 6

2 rounded teaspoons coriander seeds	4 large onions, peeled and very thinly sliced
2 rounded teaspoons cumin seeds	1 clove of garlic, peeled and finely chopped
2 rounded teaspoons ground cinnamon	1 rounded tablespoon plain flour
2 oz (50 g) lamb dripping, or butter and oil mixed	8 oz (250 g) dried apricots, soaked in 1 pint (600 ml) water for at least 6 hours
2 lb (900 g) boneless leg of lamb, trimmed and cut into 1 in (2.5 cm) pieces	salt and freshly ground black pepper

Put the coriander, cumin and cinnamon together in a pestle and mortar if you have one, to pound them. If you don't have a pestle and mortar, a small deep bowl is just as good, and I use the end of a rolling pin to pound them. You won't be able to break down the cumin entirely, but it doesn't matter, it will break down during the cooking.

Melt the dripping in a flameproof casserole (using dripping really does make a great deal of difference to the end taste of this casserole), and brown the pieces of lamb well all over, a few pieces at a time. As they brown, remove the pieces of meat to keep warm. When all the meat is browned, lower the heat under the casserole and add the sliced onions and the chopped garlic to the fat. Cook gently for 10 minutes or so, stirring all the time, until the onions are soft and transparent. Then stir in the flour and the pounded spices. Cook, stirring from time to time, for about 5 minutes. Then stir in the apricots, and the water in which they soaked, stirring all the time until the sauce boils.

Season with salt and black pepper, cover with a lid, and cook in a moderate oven, 350°F (180°C) Gas Mark 4 (bottom right-hand oven in a 4-door Aga) for 1½ hours.

Smoked Haddock Roulade with Scallops

This is another recipe using smoked haddock. It was devised by Peter MacPherson who cooks with me at Kinloch. It will keep warm, but not for too long, about 20 minutes.

Serves 8

1½ lb (700 g) smoked haddock
1½ pints (850 ml) milk and water mixed
1 onion, peeled
1 blade of mace
2 oz (50 g) butter
2 oz (50 g) plain flour
a pinch of nutmeg
a little freshly ground black pepper
4 eggs, separated
2 oz (50 g) Cheddar cheese, grated

For the filling:
8 large scallops
1 pint (600 ml) milk and water mixed
2 tablespoons white wine
2 oz (50 g) butter
1½ oz (40 g) plain flour
a pinch of grated nutmeg
freshly ground black pepper
1 tablespoon finely chopped parsley

Put the fish, mixed milk and water, the onion and the mace together in a saucepan, and over a low heat bring slowly to the boil. Simmer very gently for 5 minutes, then draw off the heat and leave for 10 minutes. Strain off and reserve the cooking liquid and remove the skin and bones from the fish.

Line a 12 × 14 in (30 × 35 cm) Swiss roll tin, or a shallow baking tray, with a piece of siliconised paper.

Melt the butter in a saucepan. Add the flour, and cook over a gentle heat for a couple of minutes. Then gradually add just over 1 pint (600 ml) of the cooking liquid, stirring all the time until the sauce comes to the boil. Take off the heat, add the seasoning and cool for 10–15 minutes. Then beat in the 4 egg yolks.

Flake the cooked fish, and stir this into the sauce. Lastly, whisk the egg whites until stiff and, using a metal spoon, fold them into the smoked haddock mixture. Sprinkle a little grated cheese on the siliconised paper and pour the smoked haddock mixture over the cheese, smoothing it evenly into the tin. Put in a moderate oven, 350°F (180°C) Gas Mark 4 (bottom right-hand oven in a 4-door Aga) for 20–30 minutes, until the mixture feels firm to the touch.

While it is cooking, put the scallops in a saucepan with the milk and water and white wine and, over a low heat, bring slowly to the simmer. Simmer for just 3 minutes – if the scallops are overcooked they will be tough. Remove from the heat, and leave for 5 minutes. Then make the sauce.

Melt the butter in a saucepan, stir in the flour, and cook for 1 minute. Then gradually strain in the liquid from the scallops, stirring all the time, until the sauce boils. Season with the nutmeg and black pepper. Remove from the heat. Cut each scallop into 4 or 5 pieces, and stir them into the sauce, together with the parsley.

When the roulade is cooked, take it out of the oven. Put a fresh piece of siliconised paper on the work surface and, taking the short sides of the paper containing the smoked haddock roulade in each hand, turn it on to the clean piece of paper. Carefully peel the old paper off the roulade, cover the surface with the scallop sauce, and roll up from the long side. Ease the roulade on to a flat plate or serving dish. Sprinkle with a little more grated cheese, and serve with a tomato salad and plain boiled brown rice.

Sole Florentine

Eggs Florentine are very good, but so is fish Florentine.
Fillets of fish are laid on a bed of cooked puréed spinach
and covered with a strong cheese sauce. You can use any
white fish, I generally use lemon sole.

Serves 6

6 fillets of sole
1½ pints (850 ml) milk
1 onion, peeled
1 blade of mace
1½ lb (700 g) frozen
   spinach, thawed
2 oz (50 g) butter
salt and freshly ground black
   pepper
freshly grated nutmeg

butter for greasing
For the sauce:
2 oz (50 g) butter
2 oz (50 g) plain flour
4 oz (125 g) Lancashire
   cheese, grated
1 rounded teaspoon made
   English mustard
salt and freshly ground black
   pepper

Put the fish in a saucepan together with the milk, onion
and mace. Over a gentle heat, bring the liquid just to the
boil, then remove the saucepan from the heat. Leave to
cool, then gently lift the fish out of the liquid and flake it.

Squeeze as much water out of the spinach as possible.
Melt the butter in a saucepan, add the spinach, salt,
pepper and a pinch of nutmeg, cover and cook gently,
stirring from time to time, for 10 minutes. If you have a
food processor, whizz the spinach to a purée. If you don't
have a food processor, chop it as finely as possible. Spread
the spinach over the bottom of a well-buttered shallow,
ovenproof dish.

Make the sauce. Melt the butter in a saucepan, stir in the
flour and cook for 1–2 minutes. Then gradually pour on
the milk from the fish, stirring all the time until the sauce
boils. Remove from the heat and stir in the grated cheese,

keeping a little aside to sprinkle over the finished dish. Stir in the mustard, salt and black pepper.

Cover the spinach with the cooked fish. Pour the cheese sauce over, and sprinkle the remaining grated cheese on top. Bake in a moderate oven, 350°F (180°C) Gas Mark 4 (bottom right-hand oven in a 4-door Aga) for 20–30 minutes, until the cheese on the top is melted and the sauce is bubbling.

Rhubarb Fudge Crumble

This is a great favourite with children and grown-ups alike. If you like, you can substitute ginger nuts for the digestive biscuits.

Serves 6

---

*1½ lb (700 g) rhubarb, cut in 1 in (2.5 cm) pieces
grated rind and juice of 1 orange
3 oz (75 g) sugar, white or brown*

*For the fudge crumble:
4 oz (125 g) butter
4 oz (125 g) demerara sugar
6 oz (175 g) digestive biscuits, crushed into crumbs
1 rounded teaspoon ground cinnamon*

Put the cut-up rhubarb in an ovenproof dish with the grated orange rind, the orange juice and the sugar. Cover the dish with a piece of foil and bake in a moderate oven, 350°F (180°C) Gas Mark 4 (bottom right-hand oven in a 4-door Aga) for about 30 minutes, until the pieces of rhubarb are just soft, but not mushy and falling apart. Cool.

Melt the butter in a saucepan, stir in the demerara sugar and the digestive crumbs and cinnamon. Cook for 5 minutes, stirring from time to time. Then cover the surface of the cooled, cooked rhubarb with this butter crumb mixture, and bake in a hot oven, 400°F (200°C) Gas Mark 6 (top right-hand oven in a 4-door Aga) for 15–20 minutes. Remove from the oven and serve either warm with vanilla ice cream, or cold with whipped cream.

Rhubarb Meringue Pie

Fruity meringue pies I love. I wish I didn't like sweet things so much.

Serves 8

5 oz (150 g) butter, chilled and cut into little bits	trimmed and cut in 1 in (2.5 cm) pieces
6 oz (175 g) plain flour	grated rind and juice of 1 orange
2 oz (50 g) icing sugar	
1 rounded dessertspoon ground ginger	3 oz (75 g) sugar
For the filling:	For the meringue:
1½ lb (700 g) rhubarb,	4 egg whites
	8 oz (225 g) caster sugar

Put the butter, flour, icing sugar and ginger in a food processor and whizz until the mixture resembles breadcrumbs. Press lightly over the sides and bottom of a flan dish about 9 in (23 cm) in diameter. (If you do not have a food processor, rub the butter into the dry ingredients, using your finger tips, until the mixture looks like breadcrumbs). Put the dish into the refrigerator for at least 30 minutes, then bake in a hot oven, 400°F (200°C) Gas Mark 6 (top right-hand oven in a 4-door Aga) for 30 minutes, or until the pastry is pale golden and cooked. Remove from the oven to cool.

Put the rhubarb, orange rind and juice and sugar together in a saucepan, cover with a lid, and cook gently until the rhubarb is just tender, but not mushy. Cool, then spoon over the cooked pastry, using a slotted spoon so that just the rhubarb goes on to the flan, and as little of the juice as possible.

Whisk the egg whites fairly stiff, then whisk in the caster sugar gradually, until the meringue is stiff and standing in peaks. Spoon over the rhubarb, covering the surface of both rhubarb and pastry entirely with meringue. Bake in a cool oven, 250°F (130°C) Gas Mark ½ (top left-hand oven in the Aga) for 20–30 minutes. Serve warm or cold, with whipped cream.

Rhubarb & Ginger Syllabub

This is for those who love ginger. I like the contrasting textures in this recipe between the smooth, creamy rhubarb mixture, the slivers of ginger through it, and the crisp butteriness of the shortbread accompanying it.

Serves 6–8

1½ lb (700 g) rhubarb, cut in small chunks
3 oz (75 g) sugar
1 pint (600 ml) double cream

1 sherry glass ginger wine
8 pieces of ginger preserved in syrup, drained

Put the rhubarb in a saucepan with the sugar. Cover the pan with a lid, put it on a gentle heat, and cook slowly for about 30 minutes, until the rhubarb is cooked and soft. Cool, then purée in a blender.

Whip the cream and the ginger wine together. Cut the ginger into slivers, and stir them into the whipped cream. Fold together the ginger cream and the rhubarb purée, and divide between glasses. Serve with Ginger Shortbread Fingers (page 94).

Ginger Shortbread Fingers

Serves 6–8

---

4 oz (125 g) butter
2 oz (50 g) icing sugar,
    sieved
4 oz (125 g) plain flour
3 oz (75 g) ground rice

1 rounded dessertspoon
    ground ginger
caster or demerara sugar to
finish

Cream the butter, adding the sieved icing sugar, and beat until really smooth. Sieve together the flour, ground rice and ginger and beat into the butter, bit by bit. Knead to a dough, then press into a greased 10 × 8 in (25 × 20 cm) baking tin, to a depth of about $\frac{1}{2}$ in (1 cm). Bake in a moderate oven, 350°F (180°C) Gas Mark 4 (bottom right-hand oven of a 4-door Aga) for 15 minutes. Sprinkle with a little caster or demerara sugar, and finish baking for another couple of minutes. Take out of the oven, cool for 5 minutes, then mark into fingers with a sharp knife. These will keep in an airtight tin for several days.

Extremely Rich Chocolate & Ginger Pudding

Oh dear, this pud is so rich, and I absolutely love it. It is a sort of heavy mousse, though really too thick and heavy to be called a mousse. You can make it up to 2 days before you want to eat it – it improves if made and left overnight. Certainly the flavour of the brandy intensifies.

---

6 oz (175 g) dark chocolate	*2–3 tablespoons brandy*
3 oz (75 g) butter	*4 eggs, separated*
2–3 oz (50–70 g) caster sugar	*6 pieces of preserved ginger, well drained*

Break the chocolate into bits, and put them in a small bowl. Put the bowl over a saucepan of simmering water until the chocolate has melted. Cool.

Beat together the butter and caster sugar, adding the sugar bit by bit and beating until the mixture is really fluffy. Stir the brandy into the cooled melted chocolate, and stir this into the butter and sugar mixture. Beat the yolks in, one by one, beating really well in between each addition. Cut the pieces of ginger into slivers, and stir them into the chocolate and brandy mixture.

Lastly, whisk the egg whites until very stiff and, using a metal spoon, fold them thoroughly into the chocolate mixture. Pour into a glass or china bowl and chill. Decorate, if you wish, with whipped cream, grated chocolate, and extra pieces of ginger.

May

In May the wild flowers are at their best, with the bluebells covering the ground. The primroses are still flourishing and the rhododendrons are out casting great banks of colour. Ever since we came to live here, the last weekend in May has been hot and lovely. Each year I hold my breath in case somehow the spell is broken and it is spent in a torrential downpour, but so far so good.

There is a bonus in May, that when it is hot weather we can all enjoy it because the annual curse of Skye and the Highlands hasn't yet got underway – that is, the dreaded midges. These tiny flying insects come in clouds from June until the first frost. They love damp weather, which we unfortunately have quite a lot of, and can make life a misery. I never know how the camping visitors to Skye can stand them.

May has seen many milestones for us locally. There was the opening several years ago of the Clan Donald museum and shop in Armadale Castle, and May 1981 we had a massive Clan Gathering. Luckily this was held during the last weekend in May so that all the visitors from America, Canada, Australia and New Zealand saw Skye at its best. Our son Hugo was christened in May – during the first weekend of the month, when it snowed! We had quite a weekend of festivities that year because, living here in Skye, you can't expect friends from afar to come just for the Christening and lunch afterwards; so they came on the Friday and left on the Monday.

During the course of that weekend we had a salmon, a present to us from Jim Fraser in Ardvasar. He started salmon fishing earlier that year, and I had never had early salmon before. They are quite different to middle-of-the-season fish, being much more moist, more gelatinous when cold, and with a superb flavour. Try them if you get the chance.

Although we live right on the sea, with a view across the Sound of Sleat to Mallaig, once one of the great fishing ports of the West coast, until recently it has been nearly impossible to buy really good fresh fish. Fish yes, but fresh, no. Then George Lawrie, the fish merchant in Mallaig, started to get a range of wonderful fresh fish. Now he rings us at Kinloch each week to see just what we would like, and we get beautiful, creamy-fresh turbot, halibut and baby plaice. He also supplies Carol and Billy Currie, who run the ever-expanding shop in Ardvasar; so now we can buy fresh haddock, sole, smoked haddock, and peppered mackerel fillets on the spot. Each year since we opened Kinloch we have got our kippers from George Lawrie; he smokes the best kippers to be found in Scotland. We also get the main part of our shellfish from George; a quick telephone call in the morning, and he puts them on the Armadale ferry for us to collect from the ferry office.

97

First Courses

Spinach and Cheese-Stuffed Pancakes
Leek and Carrot Salad
Mixed Cheese Tart
Terrine of Sausagemeat, Liver and Parsley

Main Courses

Blanquette d'Agneau
Chicken in Curry Mayonnaise
Mixed Fish Mayonnaise
Invergarry Crab Cakes
Cooking a Whole Salmon
Salmon Steaks
Cream and Chive Sauce
Salmon Kedgeree

Desserts

Cherry and Cream Yoghurt Pudding
Cherry Jam and Brandy Sauce
Cherry and Almond Tart
Chocolate and Cherry Meringue Gâteau

Spinach & Cheese-stuffed Pancakes

Serves 8

16 pancakes, see page 58
2 lb (900 g) frozen spinach, thawed
1 lb (450 g) cream cheese
1 clove of garlic, peeled and very finely chopped
salt and freshly ground black pepper
¼ rounded teaspoon grated nutmeg
butter for greasing

For the cheese sauce:
2 oz (50 g) butter
2 oz (50 g) plain flour
1 pint (570 ml) milk
1 rounded teaspoon made English mustard
6 oz (175 g) mature Lancashire cheese, grated
salt and freshly ground black pepper
a pinch of grated nutmeg

Squeeze as much water as possible out of the spinach, place it in a saucepan over a low heat and cook, stirring from time to time, for 15 minutes. Drain off any surplus juice, and cool. Put the cooled spinach into a food processor, together with the cream cheese, chopped garlic, salt, pepper and nutmeg. If you haven't got a food processor, purée all the ingredients together little by little in a blender.

Butter a shallow ovenproof dish. Divide the spinach mixture evenly between the pancakes. Roll each pancake up, and lay in rows in the dish.

To make the sauce, melt the butter in a saucepan, add the flour and cook gently, stirring, for 1–2 minutes. Then gradually add the milk, stirring all the time until the sauce boils. Stir in the mustard, seasonings and nearly all the grated cheese. Keep a little of the grated cheese aside.

Pour the sauce over the stuffed pancakes in the dish, sprinkle over the remaining grated cheese and bake in a moderately hot oven 375°F (190°C) Gas Mark 5 (bottom right-hand oven in a 4-door Aga) for 20 minutes, or until the cheese on top is melting and turning golden brown. Serve with sautéed potatoes and a tomato salad.

Leek & Carrot Salad

We make this for a first course at Kinloch and serve it with warm herb scones. The original recipe comes from Angela Fox, who used to cook at Kinloch, but I have made one or two small adaptations of my own.

Serves 6

---

2 oz (50 g) butter
6 leeks, washed, and cut in pieces about 1 in (2.5 cm) long
2 onions, peeled and very finely sliced
2 rounded teaspoons ground ginger
4 medium-sized carrots, peeled and grated

4 tomatoes, skinned, seeded and puréed in a blender
5 oz (150 g) natural yoghurt
1 rounded tablespoon finely chopped parsley
salt and freshly ground black pepper
extra chopped parsley, to serve

Melt the butter in a frying pan and add the sliced leeks. Cook over a gentle heat, stirring from time to time until the leeks are soft. Remove them from the frying pan and put them in a fairly shallow serving dish. Still on a gentle heat, put the sliced onions in the frying pan, and cook until the onions are soft and transparent. Sprinkle the ground ginger over the onions, mix well together, then remove the onions from the frying pan and distribute them evenly over the leeks in the serving dish.

Put the grated carrots in a bowl. Mix together the tomato purée, yoghurt, parsley and seasoning, and pour this over the carrots, mixing them all together well. Then put this carrot mixture over the onions and leeks, and sprinkle with more chopped parsley before serving.

Mixed Cheese Tart

This is awfully rich, but good. If you have a food processor it doesn't take a second to make; it does take a bit longer if you have to do it by hand.

Serves 8

---

12 oz (350 g) shortcrust pastry
3 oz (75 g) cream cheese
3 oz (75 g) Cheddar cheese, grated
3 oz (75 g) Brie, with the white skin cut off
3 eggs
¼ pint (150 ml) single cream

1 teaspoon Worcestershire sauce
1 large clove of garlic, peeled and finely chopped
1 rounded teaspoon mustard powder
freshly ground black pepper
1 rounded tablespoon finely chopped parsley

Roll out the pastry, and line a flan dish about 9 in (23 cm) in diameter with it. Prick the bottom of the flan all over, with a fork. Put the dish in the refrigerator for 30 minutes then bake blind in a moderate oven, 350°F (180°C) Gas Mark 4 (bottom right-hand oven in a 4-door Aga) until golden.

If you have a food processor, put in it the 3 cheeses, 1 egg, and the yolks of the remaining 2 eggs (keeping the whites in a bowl). Add the cream, Worcestershire sauce, chopped garlic, mustard powder and black pepper. Whizz the mixture together until smooth. In the separate bowl, whisk the 2 egg whites, and then fold them into the cheese mixture. Pour the lot into the cooked pastry case. Bake in a moderate oven, 350°F (180°C) Gas Mark 4 (bottom right-hand oven in the Aga) for about 25 minutes, until the filling feels just firm to the touch. Sprinkle with finely chopped parsley, and serve warm.

If you don't have a food processor, put the cheeses together in a bowl and pound and mash them together with the end of a rolling pin. Add the rest of the ingredients, lastly folding in the whisked egg whites with a metal spoon. Bake as above.

Terrine of Sausagemeat, Liver & Parsley

This is a most useful and delicious terrine. It is best if made a couple of days before it is to be eaten.

Serves 8

---

10 rashers of streaky bacon
3 bay leaves
1 lb (500 g) lamb's liver
1 lb (500 g) good pork sausagemeat
1 onion, peeled and very finely chopped

1 clove of garlic, peeled and very finely chopped
salt and freshly ground black pepper
2 rounded tablespoons finely chopped parsley

Line a 2 pint (1.1 litre) loaf tin with foil, pressing the foil right into the corners of the tin and allowing enough to cover the top of the tin. Put the 3 bay leaves in a row on the bottom of the foil. Then lay the streaky bacon rashers in rows over the bottom of the tin and up the sides.

Trim the liver of any tubes, and if you have a food processor put the liver into it with the pork sausagemeat, the chopped onion and garlic, a little salt and lots of black pepper, and the parsley. Whizz until all the ingredients are thoroughly blended.

If you don't have a food processor, ask your butcher to put the liver through his mincing machine, then, using your hands (it's a squelchy business, this), mix together thoroughly in a bowl the minced liver, sausagemeat, chopped onion, garlic, seasoning and parsley.

Pack this mixture on top of the bacon in the foil-lined tin, smoothing over the surface. Fold the foil over the top, and put the tin in a roasting tin, with cold water coming half way up the sides of the loaf tin. Bake in a moderate oven, 350°F (180°C) Gas Mark 4 (bottom right-hand oven in a 4-door Aga) for $1\frac{1}{2}$ hours.

Remove from the oven, discard the water and put the terrine in a cool place, still in its tin, with a weight on top of the foil – I use a large tin of baked beans or something similar as a weight. The next day, remove the weight and put the terrine in the refrigerator. To serve, turn the terrine out on to a serving dish, peeling the foil off. The bay leaves will be uppermost, on the streaky bacon. If you are serving it as a first course, serve with warm, brown toast.

Blanquette d'Agneau

A blanquette is traditionally made with veal, but as we can't get veal in Skye I make it with lamb.

Serves 6

---

2 lb (900 g) boneless leg of lamb, cut into 1 in (2.5 cm) cubes	2 oz (50 g) butter
1 onion, peeled and stuck with a few cloves	2 level tablespoons plain flour
2 carrots, peeled and sliced	8 oz (250 g) mushrooms, sliced
bouquet garni	2 egg yolks
salt and freshly ground black pepper	$\frac{1}{4}$ pint (150 ml) double cream
	juice of 1 lemon

Put the lamb cubes in a saucepan and cover with cold water. Put the onion stuck with cloves, the sliced carrots, the bouquet garni and a little salt and black pepper in the saucepan and bring to the boil. Then simmer gently for 45 minutes, with the pan uncovered.

In another saucepan, melt the butter. Stir in the flour and cook over a gentle heat for 1–2 minutes. Then gradually stir in 1 pint (600 ml) of the stock in which the lamb cooked. Bring to the boil and simmer, stirring, for 5 minutes. Put the sliced mushrooms in the sauce and cook gently for a further 5 minutes, stirring. Season with salt and black pepper.

Mix together the egg yolks, cream and lemon juice. Add a little of the hot sauce to this mixture, then stir the egg yolks, cream and lemon juice into the sauce; reheat gently but don't let the sauce boil again or it will curdle.

Drain the meat from the rest of the stock, put it in a warmed, ovenproof dish and pour the sauce over. Serve with rice and a green vegetable.

Chicken in Curry Mayonnaise

People rave about this cold chicken dish, out of all proportion to the effort put into it. It needs a rice salad, and we make one of brown rice, toasted flaked almonds and raisins, all tossed together in a very little French dressing. If you have a large ashet (that's Scottish for a flat plate) and pile the chicken in its sauce in the middle, you can arrange the salad round the edge of the chicken.

Serves 6

---

4 lb (1.8 kg) chicken
1 onion, peeled and quartered
1 carrot, peeled and cut in
    chunks
bouquet garni
salt
a few black peppercorns
¼ pint (150 ml) double
    cream, whipped
½ pint (300 ml) mayonnaise
    (it is fine to use a good
    bought mayonnaise for
    this recipe)

curry powder
runny honey
wine vinegar
For the rice salad:
8 oz (250 g) rice, brown if
    possible
salt
2 oz (50 g) flaked almonds
2 tablespoons raisins
2 tablespoons French
    dressing, see page 130

Put the chicken in a large saucepan and cover with water. Add the onion, carrot, bouquet garni, salt and peppercorns. Bring to the boil, cover with a lid and simmer gently for 1 hour or until the juices run clear when the point of a knife is stuck into the thigh. Leave the chicken to cool in the stock. When cold, skin it and strip all the meat from the bones.

Stir together the whipped cream, mayonnaise, 1 rounded tablespoon curry powder, 1 tablespoon honey and 1 tablespoon wine vinegar. Adjust the quantity of the ingredients to suit your own taste. Fold the sauce through the chicken meat.

Cook the rice in plenty of boiling salted water until just tender but not soft. Drain and run cold water through it until the rice is cold. Toast the flaked almonds lightly under the grill. Combine the rice, almonds, raisins and French dressing and serve with the creamy chicken.

Mixed Fish Mayonnaise

For a summery party, serve fish in a creamy mayonnaise mixture in the centre of an ashet, encircled by brown rice. Press the tomato wedges face down, as it were, into the rice.

Serves 8

---

2 lb (900 g) smoked haddock

1½ lb (700 g) white fish fillet

2 pints (1.1 litres) milk

1 onion, peeled

1 blade of mace

¼ pint (150 ml) double cream, whipped

½ pint (300 ml) good bought mayonnaise

1 rounded teaspoon curry powder

1 dessertspoon lemon juice

1 rounded tablespoon finely chopped mixed parsley and chives

6 oz (175 g) cooked shelled prawns

a few cooked mussels, shelled

2 hard-boiled eggs, shelled and chopped

2 × 2 oz (50 g) tins anchovy fillets, drained from their oil and soaked in milk for a few hours

10 oz (300 g) brown rice, cooked, cooled and drained

5 tomatoes, skinned and cut into wedges

Put the smoked and white fish together in a saucepan with the milk, onion and mace and, over a low heat, bring gently to the boil. Simmer for 2 minutes then remove from the heat. Allow the fish to cool in the milk, then drain well. Flake, removing all bones and skin.

Mix together the whipped cream, mayonnaise, curry powder, lemon juice, parsley and chives. Stir in the flaked fish, prawns, mussels and chopped hard-boiled eggs. Arrange in the middle of a flat plate or serving dish. Drain the anchovy fillets and pat them dry with kitchen paper. Cut in half lengthwise and arrange in a lattice design over the surface.

Surround the fish mayonnaise with the cooked rice. Press the tomato wedges, evenly spaced, into the rice.

Invergarry Crab Cakes

I much prefer crab to lobster. This may sound odd to those who are lobster fanatics, but unless lobster is really fresh, it can be disappointing. I also prefer both crab and lobster when served cold; I find both are almost too rich when hot. Godfrey disagrees with me over this – he loves them both hot, preferably tarted up in a sauce containing brandy, cheese, cream. I love plain dressed crab, with mayonnaise. Having said all that, there is one way I do love hot crab – that is in crab cakes. This is an American recipe, by Ellice McDonald, who has been High Commissioner of Clan Donald in the United States recently. Crab cakes are quite delicious, and can be served with a good homemade tomato sauce, or a homemade tartare sauce. They freeze well, too, for up to 3 months. Adjust the quantities of mustard and Worcestershire sauce to your taste. This quantity can make 6 large crab cakes, or more smaller ones.

1 lb (500 g) crab meat
3 slices of white bread,
  crusts removed, made into
  crumbs
2 heaped tablespoons
  mayonnaise
2 rounded teaspoons made up
  English mustard

1 tablespoon Worcestershire
  sauce
oil and butter for frying
For coating:
1 egg, beaten
6 rounded tablespoons
  breadcrumbs

Mix together the crab meat, breadcrumbs, mayonnaise, mustard and Worcestershire sauce until they are well combined. Shape the mixture into 6 rounded cakes about $\frac{3}{4}$ in (2 cm) thick, with floured hands. If you are going to freeze them, wrap them up well and freeze them at this stage; thaw before coating and frying.

To coat, dip each crab cake in beaten egg and then in breadcrumbs, and leave on a tray in the refrigerator for 2–3 hours. Then heat 4 tablespoons oil and 2 oz (50 g) butter in a large frying pan and fry the crab cakes for 3–5 minutes on each side until they are golden brown. If you need extra fat, add it as you take one lot of crab cakes out of the pan, and heat it before adding the next batch. Keep them warm on a dish containing kitchen paper to drain off any excess fat, until you are ready to eat. Serve with a good tomato sauce (see page 163) and a green salad.

Cooking a Whole Salmon

At Kinloch Hotel we have a fish kettle, but not many people have them nowadays; this is how I cook salmon without one. Gut the fish, and weigh it; calculate the cooking time at 20 minutes per 1 lb (450 g). Take a piece of foil large enough to make a parcel round the fish, and lay it flat on a table. Smear butter liberally all over the foil. Put a few sprigs of parsley and 2–3 slices of lemon on the foil, and lay the fish on this. Put a few sprigs of parsley, a couple of slices of lemon and a piece of butter inside the fish. Put sprigs of parsley, 2–3 slices of lemon and 2 pieces of butter on top of the fish, and wrap up tightly in the foil.

Put the fish in a roasting tin, with water half way up the tin. Put the tin in a moderate oven, 350°F (180°C) Gas Mark 4 (bottom right-hand oven in a 4-door Aga) for 15 minutes. Then lower the heat to 250°F (130°C) Gas Mark $\frac{1}{2}$ (or move it to the top left-hand oven in a 4-door Aga). For a fish weighing about 8 lb (3.6 kg), after 2 hours take the tin out and unwrap the fish enough to let you test to see if it is cooked, by easing up the skin with 2 forks. If the skin lifts off easily, the fish is cooked. After 2 hours it probably won't be quite ready, but it's much better to test too soon than too late, as overcooked it is dry and no amount of hollandaise sauce, or mayonnaise, can redeem it.

When it is cooked, remove it from the oven. If you are going to serve it cold, let it cool in the foil. If it is to be served hot, unwrap the foil parcel, take the skin off the side of salmon uppermost, then slide the salmon, turning it over at the same time, on to a warmed ashet, and take the skin off the other side. Have a fresh piece of buttered foil to hand, and cover the fish with this. Keep the fish warm in a cool oven until required.

An 8 lb (3.6 kg) fish will serve about 12 people. Salmon is very filling and if planning it for a party, have fairly light, fruity first courses and puds.

Salmon Steaks

I used to despise salmon steaks until Angela Fox, who cooked with us at Kinloch for 3 years, showed me how to cook them to perfection. She so inspired me that I now love them.

Serves 6

---

6 salmon steaks
at least 4 oz (125 g) butter

6 sprigs of dill weed or
parsley

Melt the butter in a shallow baking tin which is large enough to hold the steaks in a single layer. Put the steaks on the melted butter and brush the surface of each steak with the butter. Lay a piece of dill on each steak.

Put the steaks under a grill, set on half heat. Cook them under the grill, brushing frequently with the butter, until the flesh is just coming away from the bone in the centre. Turn them over once during cooking, which will take about 20 minutes in all. Take the skin off each steak before serving.

Cream & Chive Sauce

Perfect for serving with salmon, this sauce is unbelievably easy. Athough it sounds so rich, it is not nearly as heavy as a classic hollandaise sauce, made with butter and egg yolks.

Serves 6

$\frac{3}{4}$ pint (425 ml) double
cream
a squeeze of lemon juice

2 tablespoons finely chopped
chives

Put the cream into a saucepan with the lemon juice and simmer gently for 5 minutes. Just before serving stir in the finely chopped chives.

Salmon Kedgeree

Left-over salmon can be used in a variety of ways, but one of the best is kedgeree.

Serves 4–5

---

1 chicken stock cube
a pinch of saffron, optional
8 oz (250 g) long-grain white rice
3 oz (75 g) butter
1 small onion, peeled and very finely chopped

1 rounded teaspoon curry powder
4 oz (125 g) left-over cooked salmon, flaked
2 hard-boiled eggs, shelled and chopped
1 rounded tablespoon finely chopped parsley

Bring to the boil a large pan of water and dissolve in it the stock cube and a pinch of saffron if you have some. Add the rice and cook for about 12 minutes, until just tender. Drain.

Melt the butter in a saucepan, and add the finely chopped onion. Cook over a gentle heat for 5–10 minutes, until the onion is soft. Add the curry powder, and cook for 1–2 minutes, then stir in the cooked rice, the flaked salmon, and the chopped hard-boiled eggs.

Butter liberally an ovenproof dish, and put the kedgeree into the dish. Cover with 2 butter papers, or a piece of buttered foil laid over the top of the kedgeree but not tightly sealing the contents of the dish. Put the dish into a moderate oven, 350°F (180°C) Gas Mark 4 (bottom right-hand oven of a 4-door Aga) for 40 minutes, until the kedgeree is hot through. Just before serving, fork through the finely chopped parsley.

Cherry & Cream Yoghurt Pudding

This pudding is a never failing success, and gets a five star rating with adults and children alike. The recipe was given to me by April Strang Steel, who is a tremendous source of culinary inspiration. It can be made at any time of the year, using tinned black cherries, but it is best made when fresh cherries are available. It is the easiest pudding to make, and it is better made the day before it is required, therefore a recipe after my own heart.

Serves 6

½ pint (300 ml) double
   cream
1¼ lb (675 g) cherry yoghurt
8 oz (250 g) fresh cherries,
   stoned,

or 15 oz (425 g)
   tin of stoned black
   cherries, drained
demerara sugar

Whip the cream, and fold in the yoghurt. Fold in the cherries, and pour into a glass or china serving dish. Cover the surface with a layer of demerara sugar about ¼ in (5 mm) thick.

Cherry Jam & Brandy Sauce

Serve this sauce with vanilla ice cream. In the unlikely event of there being any left over, it keeps in a screw-topped jar in the refrigerator for several days.

Serves 6

---

8 oz (250 g) good cherry
   jam

4–6 tablespoons brandy, or
   cherry brandy which gives
   a sweeter sauce

Put the cherry jam into a saucepan, and warm over a low heat until runny. Stir in the brandy or cherry brandy and heat through, but don't let the sauce boil, because that will evaporate the alcohol.

Cherry & Almond Tart

We often make this tart at Kinloch during the cherry season.

Serves 8

4 oz (125 g) butter	For the filling:
3 oz (75 g) plain flour	*1½–2 lb (700–900 g)*
2 oz (50 g) icing sugar	*cherries, stoned*
2 oz (50 g) chopped or	*sugar*
flaked almonds	*1 rounded tablespoon*
a few drops of vanilla	*arrowroot*
essence	*kirsch, optional*

I make the pastry in a food processor. Put the chilled butter, cut in pieces, into the food processor, add the flour and icing sugar, and whizz until it resembles breadcrumbs. Add the almonds and vanilla essence and whizz for just a second to combine the ingredients, but not for any longer because one of the pleasures of this recipe is the contrasting textures in the pastry.

If you don't have a food processor, rub the cut-up butter into the sieved flour and icing sugar, using your finger tips. Add the chopped almonds and vanilla essence.

Press the crumby pastry lightly into a 9 in (23 cm) flan dish, and put it in the refrigerator for at least 30 minutes. Then bake it in a moderate oven, 350°F (180°C) Gas Mark 4 (bottom right-hand oven in a 4-door Aga) until it is evenly cooked and golden brown, about 30–40 minutes.

Put the cherries in a saucepan with about 1 rounded tablespoon sugar. Pour $\frac{1}{4}$ pint (150 ml) water over the cherries in the saucepan, cover the pan with a lid, and cook on a gentle heat until the cherries are soft. As they cook, the cherries will make more juice. Remove from the heat. Taste, and add a little more sugar if you wish.

Put the arrowroot into a small bowl and stir in 2 tablespoons cold water to make a smooth mixture. Stir in some juice from the cherry pan, then stir the contents of the bowl into the cherries in the pan. Replace the saucepan over a medium heat and stir until it boils.

Remove the saucepan from the heat and cool. Stir in about 2 tablespoons kirsch if you wish then spoon the cooled contents of the pan on to the almond pastry. Serve with whipped cream, slightly sweetened if you like.

Chocolate & Cherry Meringue Gâteau

I don't usually like the combination of fruit with chocolate, but somehow cherries and chocolate do go together rather well.

Serves 6–8

---

5 egg whites
10 oz (300 g) icing sugar, sieved
2 rounded tablespoons cocoa powder
4 oz (125 g) dark chocolate

$\frac{1}{2}$ pint (300 ml) double cream
8 oz (250 g) cherries, stoned, or 15 oz (425 g) tin of stoned black cherries, drained
extra icing sugar for dusting

Put the egg whites and the sieved icing sugar together in a

114

bowl, and put the bowl over a saucepan of gently simmering water. Whisk until the meringue mixture is so thick that it stands in peaks. Draw off the heat, and fold the cocoa powder into the meringue.

Put siliconised paper on 2 baking sheets and draw two 8 in (20 cm) circles round a plate, one on each piece of paper. Divide the meringue between the circles and smooth it evenly. Bake in a cool oven, 250°F (130°C) Gas Mark $\frac{1}{2}$ (top left-hand oven in a 4-door Aga) for $1\frac{1}{2}$–2 hours. Remove from the oven.

Break the chocolate into a small saucepan, add 2 tablespoons water and heat very gently until melted. Leave until cool but don't let it set again. Whip the cream, and fold in the cooled, melted chocolate. Fold the cherries into the chocolate cream. Sandwich the 2 meringue circles together with the cherry and chocolate cream and dust the top with sieved icing sugar.

June

June is the best of the summer months in Skye. The different greens of the trees and hedges are still bright and fresh looking – later, in July and August, the greens go darker and the leaves look older and leathery, and the bracken grows too high. In June the dreaded Skye midges are only just getting into full swing, so, given fine weather (which we do get in June, generally), Skye is to be enjoyed immensely. The bluebells are over, but there still lingers an occasional clump of primroses here and there and the rhododendrons are in full bloom.

The summer months bring us our thickest crop of overseas Macdonald visitors, from America, Canada, Australia and New Zealand. We are very weather-conscious, for them, and for all our visitors to Skye. It is tragic when people spend several days on the island and everything is shrouded in mist and the fine but extremely wetting rain for which Skye is famous. So we pray for good weather.

Food in June, when the weather is warm and sunny, means a variety of salads, cold soups, ice creams and soft fruits. As each new item becomes available, either in the garden or from the vegetable and fruit wholesalers, so arrives fresh inspiration. The first to arrive are gooseberries and currants. These are not around for long so I take advantage of them not only for puddings but for my storecupboard preserves. The Gooseberry and Mint Jam is my favourite with roast lamb.

First Courses

Spinach, Avocado and Bacon Salad
Cream Cheese, Yoghurt and Chive Sauce
Pineapple Jellied Ring
Mushrooms in Curry and Garlic Mayonnaise
Avocado Soup with Prawns and Yoghurt
Watercress and Lemon Soup

Main Courses

Salade Niçoise
Ham, Chicken and Cheese Salad
Chicken with Fresh Cherries in Tarragon Cream
Salami, Apple and New Potato Mayonnaise

Salad Dressings

Mayonnaise
Aïoli and Tomato Aïoli
Garlic and Herb Mayonnaise
French Dressing
Yoghurt, French Mustard and Mayonnaise Dressing

Desserts

Gooseberry Cream Pie
Elderflower Water Ice
Blackcurrant and Blackcurrant Leaf Water Ice
Blackcurrant and Redcurrant Compôte with Brown Bread Ice
Cream

Preserves

Gooseberry and Elderflower Jam
Gooseberry and Mint Jam

Spinach, Avocado & Bacon Salad

Spinach can be substituted for lettuce in any salad, and when I haven't been able to get fresh spinach in Skye (it has a nasty habit of being ready all at once in our garden, and then bolting) I have successfully substituted crisp lettuce for spinach in this recipe.

Serves 6 as a first course

6 rashers of smoked streaky bacon	*2 avocados*
12 oz–1 lb (400–500 g) fresh spinach	*4 tablespoons French dressing, see page 130*

Fry or grill the bacon rashers until they are crisp. Drain and cool them on kitchen paper, then break into 1 in (2.5 cm) bits. Wash and pat dry the spinach leaves, then tear them into smallish pieces and put them in a bowl. Sprinkle the pieces of bacon on top.

Cut the avocados in half, remove their stones, then quarter them and peel off the skin; cut the flesh into chunks. Mix together with the spinach and bacon. Pour over the French dressing and mix together thoroughly.

Cream Cheese, Yoghurt & Chive Sauce

6 oz (175 g) cream cheese	*1 tablespoon finely snipped chives*
5 oz (150 g) natural yoghurt	

Pound the cream cheese in a bowl with the yoghurt, until smooth. Stir in the chives. Serve in a bowl or sauce boat. If you have a food processor whizz together the cream cheese and yoghurt until smooth – it only takes a minute and involves no elbow grease!

Pineapple Jellied Ring

In America I have come across salads involving jelly, which are often too sweet even for me. In this jellied salad the lemon juice and the tart flavour of pineapple take the edge off the sweetness. It makes a good first course if the rest of the dinner menu is rather rich. It also looks attractive on a buffet table. You can fill the centre with either a bunch of watercress, and serve Cream Cheese, Chive and Yoghurt Sauce with it, or you can fill the centre with Bacon, Prawn and Cream Cheese Pâté (see page 80).

Serves 6–8

---

1 lemon-flavoured jelly	*15 oz (425 g) tin pineapple*
3 tablespoons lemon juice	*chunks*

Dissolve the jelly in ¾ pint (425 ml) boiling water. Stir in the lemon juice and pour into a 2 pint (1.1 litre) ring mould. Leave to cool.

Drain the pineapple and rinse with cold water to remove some of the sweetness of the syrup. When the jelly is just setting, stir in the pineapple with a fork. Leave to set in the refrigerator for several hours.

To serve fill a bowl with hot water, dip the mould into the hot water for 10 seconds, then hold a plate or serving dish over the mould and turn upside down. The jelly should slip out easily. If it doesn't, put it in the hot water for a few seconds longer. Don't leave the mould in the hot water for more than 10 seconds at a time, because it is maddening to turn out a small jellied ring surrounded by a pool of liquid melted jelly.

Mushrooms in Curry &
Garlic Mayonnaise

By cooking the mushrooms in hot butter over a high heat you reduce the shrinking which takes place when mushrooms are cooked on a lower heat.

Serves 4–6

---

1 lb (500 g) mushrooms
2 oz (50 g) butter
1 rounded dessertspoon curry
    powder

½ pint (300 ml)
    mayonnaise, see page 128
1 dessertspoon lemon juice
1 or 2 cloves of garlic, peeled
    and very finely chopped

Wipe the mushrooms and slice them. Melt the butter in a frying pan and heat until foaming. Add the mushrooms to the foaming butter, and at the same time stir in the curry powder. Cook on a high heat, stirring, for 2 minutes. Remove from the heat and cool.

Tip the mayonnaise into a bowl, and add the lemon juice and finely chopped garlic. Mix well and stir in the cooled mushrooms. Divide between the serving plates or dishes. Surround the mounds of mushrooms with some shredded lettuce if you like, and serve with warm brown rolls.

Avocado Soup with Prawns & Yoghurt

This is a pretty looking and delicious tasting summer soup. The chopped prawn garnish is optional – substitute chopped chives if you prefer. I suggest using yoghurt or sour cream to swirl on top of the soup; the more figure conscious can do like me and use yoghurt.

Serves 6–8

---

2 oz (50 g) butter
1 onion, peeled and chopped
½ green pepper, seeded and
  chopped
1½ pints (850 ml) chicken
  stock
2 avocados

juice of ½ lemon
salt and freshly ground black
  pepper
5 oz (150 g) natural yoghurt
4 oz (125 g) cooked shelled
  prawns, chopped

Melt the butter in a saucepan. Add the chopped onion and pepper and cook over a gentle heat for about 10 minutes, until the onion is transparent, and both the onion and pepper are soft. Pour on the chicken stock, bring to the boil, then draw the saucepan off the heat, and leave to cool.

Skin the avocados, remove the stones, and chop half the flesh into a blender. Pour on half the onion, pepper and chicken stock and whizz until smooth. Pour into a bowl. Then blend the remaining avocado flesh and chicken stock mixture, and pour into the bowl. Stir in the lemon juice, and salt and black pepper to taste. Put the bowl into the refrigerator until you are ready to serve.

Divide the soup between chilled soup plates, and on top of each plateful put a dessertspoon of yoghurt, with a few chopped prawns in the middle of the yoghurt. Or instead of the prawns, add some chopped chives to the yoghurt.

Watercress & Lemon Soup

This soup has a fresh flavour, and looks pretty too.

Serves 6–8

---

2 oz (50 g) butter
2 medium-sized onions,
   peeled and chopped
2 medium-sized potatoes,
   peeled and chopped
1½ pints (850 ml) chicken
   stock.

2 bunches watercress,
   washed and trimmed
1 tablespoon lemon juice
salt and freshly ground black
   pepper
¼ pint (150 ml) single
   cream

Melt the butter in a saucepan. Add the onions and cook over a gentle heat for 5 minutes, then add the chopped potatoes. Cook for a further 5 minutes, stirring from time to time to prevent them sticking. Stir in the chicken stock. Chop one bunch of watercress, and add to the saucepan. Bring the soup to the boil and simmer very gently for 30 minutes, until the potato is soft. Remove the saucepan from the heat and leave to cool.

Meanwhile, strip the leaves from the stalks of the remaining bunch of watercress, and chop them, but not too finely. Purée the cooled soup in a blender, and sieve the purée into a large bowl. Stir in the lemon juice and salt and black pepper. Stir in the chopped watercress leaves. Just before serving, divide the soup between the soup plates, and put a spoonful of cream into each plateful.

Salade Niçoise

This is what I call a main course salad, ideal for lunch. If tinned anchovies are too salty for your liking, drain them of their oil and put the contents of the tin into a small dish of milk, for as long as possible. Pat them dry with kitchen paper before cutting them into strips. This removes a lot of their saltiness.

Serves 6

---

*1 large crisp lettuce, ideally
a Cos lettuce
6 tomatoes, skinned
6 hard-boiled eggs, shelled
7 oz (200 g) tin tuna fish
8 oz (250 g) French or green
beans*

*salt
black olives
8 anchovy fillets
5 tablespoons French
dressing, see page 130
finely chopped parsley and
chives, optional*

Pull apart the washed lettuce, with your fingers. Arrange around the inside of a serving bowl. Cut both the tomatoes and hard-boiled eggs into wedges, and distribute them among the lettuce. Drain the tuna fish of its oil, and flake it into the salad. Cook the beans for just 2 minutes in boiling salted water, so that they still have a bite to them, drain them under running cold water, and put them into the salad bowl. Stone as many black olives as you like, and add them. Cut the anchovies into thin strips using a very sharp knife, and arrange them roughly in a lattice pattern over the top of the salad. Dress the salad with French dressing, to which you can add some finely chopped parsley and chives, if you like.

Ham, Chicken & Cheese Salad

This is altogether too filling for a first course, but is ideal for an all-in-one main course. It is to be found on restaurant and hotel menus throughout America, where it is offered with a variety of dressings. The only thing it generally lacks is a contrasting texture, so for a crunch I like to add dry roasted peanuts, or better still, dry roasted cashew nuts.

Serves 6

6 oz (175 g) cold cooked chicken
6 oz (175 g) cooked ham, smoked if possible
6 oz (175 g) hard cheese, Edam or Cheddar
1 large crisp lettuce
3 oz (75 g) dry roasted peanuts or cashew nuts

4–6 tablespoons salad dressing of your choice, either French dressing (page 130), or Garlic and Herb Mayonnaise (page 130)

Cut the chicken, ham and cheese into fine strips, as evenly as possible. Tear the washed lettuce into bits, using your fingers, and arrange round the side of a serving bowl.

Put the strips of chicken, ham and cheese in the middle of the bowl. Sprinkle the nuts over the whole bowl. Pour over the dressing, and gently toss the chicken, ham and cheese, trying not to break up the neatly cut strips.

Serve with warm brown rolls.

Chicken with Fresh Cherries in Tarragon Cream

I once had a jellied salad in America which was full of cherries stuffed with cream cheese. It was quite delicious and the cherries looked so neat, but I don't know how our hostess had had the time to stone and stuff so many cherries. I'm afraid that after the first half dozen I'd get fed up, eat what I'd done, and turn the rest into something else.

This is a recipe for chicken in a creamy tarragon sauce, which goes well with fresh cherries. Like all cold, creamy chicken dishes, it is good served with a rice salad.

Serves 8

---

1 cooked chicken, weighing about 4 lb (1.8 kg)
2 eggs
5 rounded tablespoons caster sugar
6 tablespoons tarragon vinegar

salt and freshly ground black pepper
¼ pint (150 ml) double cream
1 lb (500 g) cherries, stoned
finely chopped parsley

Put the eggs and caster sugar together in a bowl, and put the bowl over a saucepan of gently simmering water. Beat the eggs (using an electric hand-beater if you have one) until they are thick and pale. Remove the bowl from the heat and continue beating, adding the vinegar gradually, and a pinch each of salt and pepper. At this stage you can put the tarragon dressing in a sealed container and keep it in the refrigerator for at least a week.

Strip the flesh off the cooked chicken, and cut into pieces as neatly as possible. Discard the skin and bones.

Whip the cream and fold it together with the tarragon dressing. Mix together the stoned cherries, the tarragon cream and the chicken, and put the salad on a flat plate or shallow serving dish. Sprinkle some finely chopped parsley over the surface.

Salami, Apple & New Potato Mayonnaise

I first had this delicious salad at lunch with Araminta Dallmeyer. It had actually been concocted by Margaret Taylor, who is Minty's right hand while she works for the National Trust of Scotland. Our children love it.

Serves 6–8

12 oz (350 g) salami in one piece, if possible German peppered salami
3 dessert apples
8 medium-sized new potatoes, cooked
1 clove of garlic, peeled and finely chopped

6 tablespoons good mayonnaise, see page 128
freshly ground black pepper, if you are not using peppered salami
finely chopped parsley

Skin the salami and cut it into small chunks. Core the apples, and cut into $\frac{1}{2}$ in (1 cm) chunks, but don't take the skin off the apples. Skin the potatoes and cut into chunks the same size.

Stir the garlic into the mayonnaise. Mix together the salami, potatoes and apples with the garlic mayonnaise and season with pepper if necessary. Pile the salad into a serving bowl, and sprinkle the top with finely chopped parsley.

Mayonnaise

This can be made in a blender or food processor, and takes only a couple of minutes. It keeps in a screw-topped jar or covered container in the refrigerator for a week or two. Personally I find that using all olive oil gives too pronounced a taste, so I like to use part olive oil and part sunflower seed oil; this is purely a matter of personal preference.

Makes about ½ pint (300 ml)

---

1 whole egg
1 egg yolk
1 rounded teaspoon mustard powder
1 rounded teaspoon salt
1½ rounded teaspoons sugar

about 12 grinds of black pepper
¼ pint (150 ml) sunflower seed oil
2 fl oz (50 ml) olive oil
2–3 tablespoons wine vinegar

Put the egg, yolk, mustard powder, salt, sugar and pepper into the blender or food processor, and whizz for a second. Slowly, drip by drip to start with, add some of the oil. Then, tablespoon by tablespoon, add the wine vinegar; taste before you add the third tablespoon, because 2 spoonsful may be enough for your taste. Slowly add the rest of the oil, at a steady trickle until it is all used up.

If things go wrong, which usually only happens when you are in a tremendous rush, don't despair. The whole thing can be redeemed by pouring the thin, curdled mayonnaise into a jug, and putting an extra egg yolk into the blender, whizzing, and adding the curdled contents of the jug very slowly, drip by drip, until all used up. This gives perfect mayonnaise.

Aïoli

This is just mayonnaise with garlic added. The quantity of garlic added depends on your liking for it. I add 2 cloves to the mayonnaise quantities given on page 128.

Tomato Aïoli

I like to make Tomato Aïoli, by adding tomato purée and the chopped flesh of some fresh tomatoes.

---

1 whole egg	*¼ pint (150 ml) sunflower*
1 egg yolk	*seed oil*
1 rounded teaspoon mustard	*2–3 tablespoons wine*
powder	*vinegar*
1 rounded teaspoon salt	*2 cloves of garlic, peeled and*
1½ teaspoons sugar	*chopped*
about 12 grinds of black	*2 rounded teaspoons tomato*
pepper	*purée*
	3 tomatoes

Into the blender or food processor put the egg, egg yolk, mustard powder, salt, sugar and black pepper. Whizz. Then add the oil drip by drip. Add the wine vinegar. Add the chopped garlic, it will break down in the blending. Add the tomato purée.

Drop the tomatoes into a saucepan of boiling water for 2–3 seconds then nick the skins with a knife and remove them. Cut the tomatoes in half, and remove all the seeds. Cut the flesh into quite small pieces, and stir into the aïoli.

Garlic & Herb Mayonnaise

½ pint mayonnaise, see page
  128
1–2 cloves of garlic, peeled
  and finely chopped

2 rounded tablespoons finely
  chopped mixed fresh
  herbs, e.g. chives,
  parsley, fennel and chervil

Blend the garlic and herbs into the mayonnaise, adding as
much garlic as you like.

French Dressing

As with mayonnaise, I find that using all olive oil gives too
heavy a taste to the dressing, so I combine olive oil with
sunflower seed oil.

Makes about ¼ pint (150 ml)

---

2 rounded teaspoons caster
  sugar
1 rounded teaspoon salt
about 12 grinds of black
  pepper

1 rounded teaspoon mustard
  powder
2 tablespoons wine vinegar
4 tablespoons sunflower seed
  oil
2 tablespoons olive oil

Put all the ingredients together in a screw-topped jar, and
shake until thoroughly mixed.

You can add to the above dressing 2 tablespoons finely
chopped parsley, or parsley and chives, or mixed fresh
herbs finely chopped.

Yoghurt, French Mustard & Mayonnaise Dressing

This dressing is lower in calories than mayonnaise, because of the natural yoghurt content. It makes a refreshing change from mayonnaise and French dressing.

2 rounded teaspoons French mustard
1 clove of garlic, peeled and very finely chopped

4 tablespoons natural yoghurt
2 tablespoons mayonnaise

Mix all the ingredients together thoroughly, and pour over the salad.

Gooseberry Cream Pie

This is one of my favourite puddings. Sadly, it doesn't rate very highly with the rest of my family who are not gooseberry lovers. It goes down well, however, at Kinloch, so I plunder any which happens to be left over at the hotel.

Serves 6–8

4 oz (125 g) butter, chilled
4 oz (125 g) plain flour
2 oz (50 g) icing sugar
a few drops of vanilla essence

For the filling:
about 12 oz (350 g) gooseberries, topped and tailed
2 eggs
1 egg yolk
3 oz (75 g) caster sugar
7 fl oz (200 ml) double cream

Make the pastry in a food processor, by cutting up the hard butter into pieces, putting them into the processor along with the flour, icing sugar and vanilla essence, and whizzing until all the ingredients are blended and resemble fine breadcrumbs.

If you don't have a food processor, rub the butter into the flour and icing sugar, using your finger tips, then add the vanilla essence.

Lightly pat the crumby pastry into an 8–9 in (20–23 cm) flan dish, and put the dish into the refrigerator for at least 30 minutes – longer, if possible. Bake in a moderate oven, 350°F (180°C) Gas Mark 4 (bottom right-hand oven in a 4-door Aga) until the pastry is golden brown all over, 20–30 minutes. If the pastry slips down the side of the tin whilst cooking, press it back using the back of a spoon. Remove from the oven and cool.

Put the gooseberries over the surface of the cooked pastry. Beat together the eggs, yolk, caster sugar and cream until well mixed. Pour over the gooseberries, and bake in a moderate oven, 350°F (180°C) Gas Mark 4 (bottom right-hand oven in a 4-door Aga) until the filling is just firm to the touch, about 30 minutes.

Elderflower Water Ice

This delicately flavoured water ice makes a refreshing finale to a meal, especially if the first course and main course are rather rich.

Serves 6–8

rind and juice of 2 lemons	*5 or 6 heads of elderflower*
6 oz (175 g) granulated	
sugar	

Put the lemon rind, sugar and 1 pint (600 ml) water into a saucepan, and stir over a gentle heat until the sugar has dissolved completely. Then boil for 5 minutes. Remove the saucepan from the heat, add the lemon juice and the elderflower heads, stirring them into the syrup. Leave to cool completely.

Strain the liquid through a sieve into a plastic container for freezing; cover, and freeze for 2–3 hours, until it is mushy, then either whisk with a rotary or electric beater, or better still put the half-frozen ice into a food processor and whizz. Freeze again, and repeat the beating process. Do this 3 or 4 times – the water ice will increase in volume and become opaque and smooth, as the ice crystals are broken down. It will be easy to spoon out of the container straight from the deep freeze when it is required.

Blackcurrant & Blackcurrant Leaf Water Ice

Adding the blackcurrant leaves to the syrup of this water ice enhances the flavour.

Serves 6–8

---

8 oz (225 g) granulated sugar	*a handful of blackcurrant leaves*
rind and juice of 2 lemons	*8 oz (225 g) blackcurrants*

Put 1 pint (600 ml) water, 6 oz (175 g) sugar and the lemon rind together in a saucepan over a gentle heat, and stir until the sugar has dissolved completely. Then boil fast for 5 minutes. Remove from the heat, and stir in the lemon juice and the blackcurrant leaves. Leave until cold.

Put the blackcurrants, the remaining sugar and 4 tablespoons water together in a saucepan – don't bother to top and tail the blackcurrants, they will be puréed and sieved later. Cook over a gentle heat until the currants are soft. Cool, purée in a blender and sieve, to give a really smooth purée.

Strain the cold lemon and blackcurrant leaf syrup, and stir it into the blackcurrant purée. Put this into a plastic container and freeze for 2–3 hours, until it is freezing round the edges and mushy in the middle. Beat it with a rotary whisk or electric hand-beater, or better still, put it into a food processor and whizz. Return the purée to the plastic container, refreeze, and after a couple of hours repeat the beating. Do this 3–4 times, and you will have a smooth water ice, which is easy to spoon out of the container straight from the deep freeze.

Blackcurrant & Redcurrant Compôte with Brown Bread Ice Cream

The brown bread ice cream recipe was given to me by Jean Lindsay and is by far the best version of this delicious ice cream that I have come across. We make it with the breadcrumbs from our own brown bread, which we bake every day at Kinloch.

Serves 6–8

---

3 oz (75 g) blackcurrants
3 oz (75 g) redcurrants
3 oz (75 g) sugar
For the ice cream:
3 oz (75 g) wholewheat
  breadcrumbs

2 oz (50 g) granulated
  sugar
¾ pint (425 ml) double
  cream
3 oz (75 g) icing sugar,
  sieved
½ teaspoon vanilla essence

Make the ice cream first. Toast the breadcrumbs until they are golden and leave to cool. Then stir the sugar into 3 tablespoons water and heat gently until dissolved. Then boil for 2 minutes. Stir the toasted crumbs into the syrup. They will become hard as they cool, but any that form sugary lumps can be bashed back into crumbs with the end of a rolling pin.

Whip the cream with the icing sugar and vanilla essence and stir in the cooled, sugar-coated crumbs. Put the mixture in a plastic container and freeze. Remove the ice cream from the deep freeze and put it in the refrigerator just before dinner starts; bring it out to room temperature as you serve the main course.

To make the compôte, top and tail the currants and put them in a pan with the sugar. Place the pan over gentle heat and the juice will begin to flow as the currants heat.

When the sugar has dissolved and the currants are soft, remove from the heat and leave to cool. Turn into a glass bowl for serving with the brown bread ice cream.

Gooseberry & Elderflower Jam

Elderflower has one of the most delicate flavours. The clusters of tiny, creamy flowers give a flavour faintly reminiscent of muscat grapes that goes well with gooseberries, and also with strawberries. This jam is delicious, and keeps the flavour of elderflower with you all year (as with strawberry and elderflower jam, in the next chapter).

Makes about 6½ lb (2.9 kg)

3 lb (1.4 kg) gooseberries, topped and tailed	*2 handfuls elderflower heads 4 lb (1.8 kg) granulated sugar*

Put the gooseberries and 1 pint (600 ml) water in a saucepan, and simmer gently until the fruit is just soft. Gently strip the tiny heads of elderflower from the stalks, and put them in the saucepan. Add the sugar to the pan, and stir until the sugar is completely dissolved. Then boil rapidly. After 10–15 minutes' fast boiling, draw the pan off the heat, and put a small spoonful of jam on a cold saucer. Leave until completely cold, and then gently push the surface of the jam with your finger tip. If the jam wrinkles, it will set. If it is still runny, put the saucepan back on the heat and boil rapidly for 5 minutes before testing again. Always take the saucepan off the heat while you are testing.

Pot into warmed jars, and cover with a disc of waxed paper. Seal with cellophane and rubber bands when the jars are quite cold.

Gooseberry & Mint Jam

Serve this with lamb, as a change from redcurrant jelly or mint jelly.

Makes about 6½ lb (2.9 kg)

---

3 lb (1.4 kg) gooseberries, topped and tailed

4 stems of mint

4 lb (1.8 kg) granulated sugar

¼ pint (150 ml) white wine vinegar

2 rounded tablespoons finely chopped mint

Put the gooseberries, ¾ pint (425 ml) water, and the stems of mint into a saucepan, and simmer until the gooseberries are soft. Add the sugar and stir until completely dissolved, then boil rapidly for about 15 minutes. Draw the pan off the heat, and test to see if it has reached setting point, by putting a small spoonful of jam on to a saucer, and leaving it until completely cold. If the surface of the jam wrinkles when you push it gently with your finger tip, the jam will set. If it is still runny, boil the jam rapidly for a further 5 minutes, then test again in the same way.

When it has reached setting point, fish out the stalks of mint with a wooden spoon, and then stir in the wine vinegar and finely chopped mint. Pot into warmed jars, cover with discs of waxed paper, and seal with cellophane and rubber bands when the jars are quite cold.

July

Scottish schools break up much earlier than the English, so the beginning of July heralds the start of our summer holidays. This means that we are torn between being – hopefully – extremely busy at the hotel, and a feeling of guilt that the girls are on holiday and we should be doing more together as a family. This must be common to all parents involved in hotel life, and is where the rest of our family are such a God-send. The children go off happily to stay with either aunts or grandparents, or the relations come and stay with us. Friends with their families come to stay with us too. These good friends know the existence we lead during the busy months and don't mind, occasionally, helping out – perhaps washing up, or doing some flowers.

But despite the rush, during the holidays we have lots of barbecues. Skye, together with the North of Scotland generally, enjoys long hours of daylight at this time of year. In fact in June and July, given fine weather, there are really only two or three hours of complete darkness during the short nights.

To my mind, barbecues are the ideal form of entertaining, because you are bound to a certain measure of informality. At one time we did all our barbecuing in a small pit with a fireproof brick surrounding, and an old boot scraper over the charcoal to put the food on whilst cooking. We have now invested in a large barbecue with a huge domed lid, which means that should the weather turn inclement, our supper needn't be washed out.

Fresh soft fruit is available in abundance during July, especially strawberries. The first strawberries are such a treat, that it is a shame to do anything more than pile them on an ashet, dust liberally with caster sugar, and eat them with cream.

Later I like to blend them with other flavours to ring the changes. Lemon and orange both bring out the delicate strawberry flavour; coffee flavour and strawberry go together well, too, and lovely, delicate elderflower complements the strawberries exquisitely. All of these flavours feature in the strawberry recipes which follow.

First Courses

Tomatoes Stuffed with Tuna Fish Pâté
Courgettes and Mushrooms in Cream and Soy Sauce
Brown Garlic Rolls
Mint, Pea and Lettuce Soup
Avocado, Melon and Tomato Salad

Barbecue Food

Marinated Chicken Pieces
Scallop and Bacon Kebabs
Kidney and Mushroom Kebabs
Pork and Orange Kebabs
Cold Barbecue Sauce
Barbecued Salmon
Hot Barbecue Sauce

Salads

Potato Salad
Tomato and Orange Salad

Desserts

Strawberries with Lemon Syllabub
Strawberries with Crème Anglaise
Strawberry Compôte with Coffee Ice Cream
Strawberry and Orange Compôte with Brown Sugar Meringues

Preserves

Strawberry and Elderflower Jam

Tomatoes Stuffed with Tuna Fish Pâté

This is one of my favourite summer first courses.

Serves 6

---

allow 1 tomato per person, if large, if they are rather small, allow 2 each
7 oz (200 g) tin tuna fish, drained

12 oz (350 g) cream cheese
1 clove of garlic, peeled and finely chopped
1 tablespoon lemon juice
freshly ground black pepper
dash of Tabasco
a few black olives, and some chopped parsley, for garnish

Carefully slice the bottom off each tomato – they will stand up firmly on their stalk ends. Using a small teaspoon, scoop the seeds out of the tomato, and as much of the core as possible, trying not to tear the skin. Put the tomatoes 'face down' on a piece of kitchen paper to drain while you prepare the stuffing.

If you have a food processor, put all the other ingredients into it, and whizz until smooth. If you don't have a food processor, put the tuna fish, cream cheese and garlic, lemon juice, pepper and Tabasco into a deep bowl and, using the end of a rolling pin, pound all together until the mixture is as smooth as you can get it. If you make the pâté this way, fill each tomato with the pâté using a teaspoon. If you have a food processor, your pâté will be much smoother, and a neater result is achieved by filling the tomatoes using a piping bag with a wide, star nozzle.

Stone the olives, cut in half and stick 2 halves on top of each stuffed tomato. Dust them all with chopped parsley.

Courgettes & Mushrooms in Cream & Soy Sauce

We grow courgettes, and after the first of the season, they tend to grow in such abundance that I rack my brains for ideas for cooking them. This is a recipe of my mother's; it is easy, good, and can either be used as a first course, or as a vegetable accompaniment for the main course.

Serves 6

---

about 10 courgettes, 5–6 in (12.5–15 cm) long
8 oz (250 g) mushrooms
2 oz (50 g) butter

½ pint (300 ml) single cream
2 tablespoons soy sauce
salt and freshly ground black pepper

Cut the courgettes into 1 in (2.5 cm) pieces and throw away the ends. Slice the mushrooms.

Melt the butter in a wide, shallow pan, ideally a large frying pan. Put the courgettes into the melted butter, and cook for about 15–20 minutes, over a gentle heat, shaking the pan from time to time, to turn the pieces of courgette as they cook. Stir in the sliced mushrooms and the cream and soy sauce. Season with salt and pepper, and raise the heat under the pan. Cook, with the cream boiling, for 5 minutes, then turn into a heated serving dish.

Brown Garlic Rolls

These rolls were the idea of Araminta Dallmeyer.

Serves 6

---

4 oz (125 g) soft butter
2 cloves of garlic, peeled and
   finely chopped

salt and freshly ground black
   pepper
6 coarse wholemeal rolls

Mash together the butter, garlic, salt and pepper. Cut each roll in half, and spread liberally with the garlic butter. Put the rolls on a large piece of foil and pinch the edges of the foil together to make a parcel. Put in a warm oven, 325°F (170°C) Gas Mark 3 (top left-hand oven in a 4-door Aga) for 30 minutes.

Mint, Pea & Lettuce Soup

Serves 6

---

2 oz (50 g) butter
2 onions, peeled and chopped
1 clove of garlic, peeled and
  chopped, optional
2 potatoes, peeled and cut
  into small pieces
2 handfuls of lettuce leaves –
  the outer leaves are fine for
  soup
4 oz (125 g) shelled fresh or
  frozen peas

1½ pints (850 ml) chicken
  stock
salt and freshly ground black
  pepper
handful of mint leaves,
  stripped from the stalks
6 tablespoons single cream
finely chopped parsley

Melt the butter in a saucepan, add the onions, garlic and
potatoes and cook over gentle heat for about 10 minutes,
stirring from time to time to prevent sticking. Add the
lettuce and peas to the saucepan and stir in the stock. Bring
to the boil and simmer very gently for 30 minutes, until the
pieces of potato are soft. Remove the saucepan from the
heat and leave to cool.

Purée the cooled vegetables in a blender, together with
the mint leaves. Season with salt and freshly ground black
pepper, pour the puréed soup into a bowl and chill. To
serve, spoon the soup into soup plates, pour a spoonful of
cream on top of each plateful and add a sprinkling of finely
chopped parsley.

Avocado, Melon & Tomato Salad

Serves 6

6 tomatoes
2 avocados
1 tablespoon lemon juice
½ medium-sized melon

6 tablespoons French
  dressing, see page 130
4–6 leaves of mint,
  applemint if possible,
  chopped

To skin the tomatoes, hold them, one by one, skewered on a fork in a saucepan of boiling water for about 30 seconds each. The skins will easily slip off. Cut the tomatoes in half, scoop out the seeds, and cut each half in 3 wedges. Put them in a bowl, a glass bowl if possible, because this is a very pretty salad.

Skin the avocados, remove the stones, and cut the flesh into chunks. Sprinkle some lemon juice over the pieces, to help prevent them from going brown. Cut the skin off the melon, discard the seeds and cut the flesh into chunks.

Mix together in the bowl, the avocado, melon and tomato, pour on the French dressing and stir in the chopped mint leaves. Don't mix the salad more than 30 minutes or so before serving, because the melon juice dilutes the French dressing. Serve with Brown Garlic Rolls.

Barbecues

All these ideas for cooking on a barbecue can equally well be cooked under an indoor grill.

If you are barbecuing, there are one or two things to bear in mind. Remember to light the fire early, because the fire takes quite a while to burn down from the leaping flame stage to the white glow which is the signal that the fire is ready for cooking. If you cook while the fire is still burning brightly, you will have a cremated dinner.

Another thing to beware of when barbecuing is having half the dinner ready, and then finding there is a long delay before the next half is cooked. Barbecue-cooked food will keep warm satisfactorily, so cook in good time, and keep the first batch warm in a cool oven.

There is a wide variety of food which can be barbecued but, although the flavour of charcoal-grilled food is absolutely delicious, it is a drying form of cooking. One way to counteract this is to marinate the food, for anything from a few hours to a couple of days. Marinades are fun to experiment with and chicken especially benefits from a good soak in a tasty mixture.

Marinated Chicken Pieces

This marinade does rather resemble a witch's brew; I think it must be the soy sauce which gives it a bluish hue, but the chicken tastes delicious!

Serves 6

6 boneless chicken breasts	1 rounded tablespoon curry powder
For the marinade:	
14 fl oz (400 ml) sunflower seed oil	2 cloves of garlic, peeled and chopped

7 fl oz (200 ml) dry white wine	*2 rounded tablespoons muscovado sugar*
2 tablespoons soy sauce	*lots of freshly ground black pepper*

Mix the marinade ingredients together. Put the chicken pieces in and leave covered in the refrigerator for 24–48 hours turning them occasionally.

Remove the chicken from the marinade and pat dry with kitchen paper before putting the chicken pieces on the barbecue. Cook for 5–10 minutes each side.

Scallop & Bacon Kebabs

Shellfish and bacon complement each other well, and for barbecuing the bacon serves a dual purpose because it prevents the scallops from drying out whilst they are cooking. You can substitute big prawns for the scallops, if you prefer.

Serves 6

30 medium scallops or 15 very large ones, halved	*15 rashers streaky bacon, halved*
	sunflower seed oil

Wrap each scallop, or piece of scallop, in a piece of bacon, and push on to a skewer, 5 to a skewer. Brush each skewerful with oil before cooking. The kebabs take about 20 minutes to cook on the barbecue, turning them so that they cook evenly. Serve them with Tomato Aïoli, page 129.

Kidney & Mushroom Kebabs

Kebabs are very versatile. You can make all sorts of delicious meat and vegetable combinations, stick them on a skewer and barbecue them. You can buy beautiful kebab skewers or use ordinary kitchen skewers; the proper skewers are easier to handle than kitchen skewers as they have larger ends to hold on to, and their blades are broader and flatter, which holds the food in place better. Lamb's kidneys make delicious kebabs.

Serves 6

---

15 lambs' kidneys	*18 mushrooms*
15 rashers streaky bacon, halved	*sunflower seed oil*

Skin and core the kidneys and cut each kidney in half. Wrap each kidney half in streaky bacon, and push them on the skewers, alternating with a mushroom, until the skewers are evenly filled. Brush with oil and cook on the barbecue, turning during cooking, for 20–30 minutes.

These kebabs are good served with a mustardy mayonnaise. Follow the recipe for mayonnaise on page 128, but increase the dry mustard quantity to 2 rounded dessertspoons.

Pork & Orange Kebabs

Serves 6

---

3 pork fillets, about 8 oz (250 g) each	*7 fl oz (200 ml) fresh (or diluted frozen) orange*
2 red peppers	*juice*

18 mushrooms
2 medium-sized onions,
   peeled
For the marinade:
14 fl oz (400 ml) sunflower
   seed oil

2 cloves of garlic, peeled and
   chopped
a few strips of orange rind
a few sprigs of rosemary
freshly ground black pepper

Mix all the marinade ingredients together. Cut the pork fillets into 1 in (2.5 cm) chunks. You want about 5 pieces per person. Put them in the marinade, cover and refrigerate for at least 12 hours.

Cut the red peppers in half and scoop out the seeds. Cut each half in 3. Cut the onions in quarters, then cut the quartered onions in half again. Put these large pieces of onion into a saucepan of cold water, bring to the boil, and simmer for 3 minutes. Add the pieces of red pepper, cook for 2 more minutes, then drain and cool.

Drain the pieces of pork from the marinade. Thread them on to 6 skewers, alternating with a piece of onion, a piece of red pepper, and a mushroom, until the skewers are evenly filled. Cook on the barbecue, turning the kebabs so that they cook evenly, for 20–30 minutes.

Cold Barbecue Sauce

This sauce goes well with all meaty barbecued food.

Serves 4–6

¼ pint (150 ml) double
   cream

3 tablespoons Branston
   pickle

Whip the cream, and stir into it the Branston pickle.

Barbecued Salmon

This is the most delicious way of cooking salmon that I know. The charcoal flavour penetrates the foil parcel, giving the salmon the most exquisite flavour. My mother was rather dubious about this until one evening when she, my father and some friends were staying. It was pronounced the most deliciously cooked salmon eaten by any of them! Praise indeed . . .

As there are many ways to deal with cold left-over salmon, as well as eating it just as it is, do not be put off if you have a fish rather larger than you need to feed the number of people at dinner.

Put the fish on a piece of foil sufficiently large to wrap the fish completely. Butter the foil, and put two or three pieces of lemon and stalks of parsley inside the fish. Put the foil parcel on the barbecue, turn it over after 15 minutes' cooking, and give it a further 15 minutes. Carefully unwrap the foil, lift a piece of skin in the middle of the fish, to see how it's getting on. It won't be cooked unless it is a small fish of around 5 lb (2.3 kg), but during the cooking time, which will be between 45 minutes and 1 hour, turn the parcel of fish, so that it cooks for an even time on each side.

I like to serve barbecued salmon with Tomato Aïoli (page 129).

Hot Barbecue Sauce

This is also for serving with meaty barbecued food.

Serves 6

4 tablespoons sunflower seed oil

1 large onion, peeled and thinly sliced

1 clove of garlic, peeled and finely chopped

15 oz (425 g) tin tomatoes

1 rounded tablespoon soft dark brown sugar

4 tablespoons tomato ketchup

2 tablespoons wine vinegar, white or red

a dash of Worcestershire sauce

Put the oil in a saucepan over a gentle heat. Add the onion and garlic and cook until the onion is soft and transparent. Add the contents of the tin of tomatoes, the brown sugar, tomato ketchup, wine vinegar and Worcestershire sauce. Stir well and simmer for 30–40 minutes, uncovered.

Potato Salad

This recipe was given to me by my American Aunt Janie. Whenever I make it, it is fallen upon with cries of glee, and any which happens to be left over has a habit of vanishing mysteriously from the larder.

Serves 6–8

10–12 potatoes (new or old)

3 hard-boiled eggs

2 sticks of celery

6 spring onions

8 rounded tablespoons mayonnaise

2 rounded tablespoons finely chopped parsley

salt and freshly ground black pepper

Boil the potatoes in their skins, in salted water until cooked, but only just. When they are cool enough to handle, peel the skin off them, and cut them into neat little chunks.

Shell the hard-boiled eggs, and chop them into pieces. Wash the sticks of celery and slice them as thinly as possible. Slice the spring onions very thinly.

Mix together the mayonnaise and parsley and put the potatoes, hard-boiled eggs, celery, spring onions and parsley mayonnaise together in a serving bowl Sprinkle with a little salt, and lots of black pepper, and mix all together thoroughly, but gently so as not to break up the pieces of potato.

The finely chopped celery gives a slight crunch through the salad, which provides a pleasing contrast to the potato and egg.

Tomato & Orange Salad

I love tomatoes. Beware when making a salad that if they are dressed with a French dressing too soon before they are to be eaten, they make a lot of juice and so dilute the dressing.

Serves 6

---

1 lb (500 g) tomatoes
4 oranges
about 4 tablespoons French dressing, see page 130

1 rounded tablespoon finely chopped chives

Skin the tomatoes, by holding them one at a time skewered on a fork, in a saucepan of simmering water, keeping the tomatoes in the water for about 30 seconds. The skins will then slip off easily.

Cut each tomato in half, then cut each half in three wedges, removing as many of the pips as possible. Put them in a shallow serving dish. Cut the skin off the oranges, using a serrated knife and removing as much of the pith as possible with the skin. Cut in between the membranes, towards the centre of each orange, to give segments.

Gently mix the wedges of tomato and orange segments together with the French dressing. Sprinkle the finely chopped chives over the top before serving.

Strawberries with Lemon Syllabub

Not only does lemon syllabub go so much better with strawberries than plain cream and sugar, but this recipe is a way of making not very many strawberries into a delicious pudding for several people.

Serves 6

---

8 oz (250 g) fresh strawberries	*juice and grated rind of 2 lemons*
½ pint (300 ml) double cream	*1 sherry glass of white wine*
	2 oz (50 g) caster sugar

Slice the strawberries and divide evenly between 6 glasses.

Whip the cream, gradually adding the lemon juice, rind, white wine and sugar. When the cream mixture is thick, spoon over the sliced strawberries in the glasses, and stir the strawberries up through the lemon syllabub. Chill for several hours before serving.

Strawberries with Crème Anglaise

This is how we serve strawberries when they are in perfect condition. Crème anglaise, which is a cold, vanilla-flavoured custard made with cream, has a more pleasing texture than plain cream.

Serves 6

---

1 lb (500 g) strawberries	*1 vanilla pod, or a few drops of vanilla essence*
caster sugar	*3 egg yolks*
½ pint (300 ml) double cream	

154

Put the strawberries on a small ashet or flat plate, piled up, and dust them with some caster sugar.

Put the cream and vanilla pod into a saucepan, and put the pan on a low heat. Beat together the egg yolks and 1 rounded tablespoon caster sugar until thick and pale. When the cream is just forming a skin, pour it on to the yolks and sugar mixture, mixing together well. Then pour this back into the saucepan and, over a very gentle heat, stir until the sauce just coats the back of the wooden spoon. Do not be tempted to raise the heat under the pan, because the sauce will curdle. If this should happen, immediately pour the sauce into a bowl, and whisk with a rotary whisk as it cools.

When the sauce coats the back of the spoon thinly, draw the saucepan off the heat and pour the sauce through a sieve into a bowl. Leave to cool. As it cools, it will thicken. This sauce is fine made the day before it is required. Hand it round in a bowl or sauce boat for spooning over the strawberries.

Strawberry Compôte with Coffee Ice Cream

This is the best ice cream recipe I have ever come across. It was given to me by Caroline Fox, an inspired cook. It doesn't need any beating during freezing, and it has a lovely smooth texture.

Serves 6

1 lb (500 g) strawberries	*4 eggs, separated*
1 rounded tablespoon caster sugar	*4 oz (125 g) icing sugar, sieved*
For the ice cream:	*½ pint (300 ml) double cream, whipped*
1 rounded tablespoon instant coffee	

First make the ice cream. Dissolve the instant coffee in 2 tablespoons boiling water and leave to cool. Beat the egg yolks with 1 oz (25 g) of the sieved icing sugar, until the mixture is pale. Stir this yolk mixture into the whipped double cream.

Whisk the egg whites until fairly stiff, then add, spoonful by spoonful, the remaining sieved icing sugar, whisking all the time until you have a stiff meringue.

By now, the coffee will be cool, so stir it into the cream and yolk mixture. Fold the meringue mixture into the coffee-flavoured cream, pour this into a plastic container, cover, and freeze.

Slice the strawberries into a bowl, and sprinkle with the sugar. Do this several hours before you want to eat, so that they form some syrup in the bowl. Serve with spoonsful of the coffee ice cream.

Strawberry & Orange Compôte with Brown Sugar Meringues

Strawberries and oranges go well together. I suggest you serve them with crunchy brown sugar meringues, with an orange flavoured cream filling. They go down very well on the menu at Kinloch.

Serves 6

---

8 oz (250 g) strawberries
4 oranges
1 tablespoon caster sugar
For the meringues:
4 egg whites
4 oz (125 g) granulated sugar

4 oz (125 g) demerara sugar
½ pint (300 ml) double cream
1 oz (25 g) caster sugar
finely grated rind of 1 orange

To make the meringues, put the egg whites in a bowl, and whisk until fairly stiff, then gradually whisk in the granulated and demerara sugars. Put a sheet of siliconised paper on a baking tray and, using 2 spoons, scoop the meringue on to the paper, making the shapes as even as possible. Bake the meringues in a cool oven, 200°F (100°C) Gas Mark ¼ (top left-hand oven in a 4-door Aga) for 3–4 hours. Remove from the oven, cool on the paper, then gently lift them off. (At this stage you can store them in an airtight tin.)

Slice the strawberries into a bowl. Cut the peel off the oranges using a serrated knife, and remove as much of the pith as possible. Catch any juice that oozes from the oranges as you peel them, put this juice in the bowl with the strawberries. Slice the oranges towards their centres, cutting between the membranes, so you have skinless segments. Mix these segments with the strawberries, and sprinkle with the caster sugar.

Whip the cream, together with the caster sugar and orange rind, until stiff. Sandwich together the meringues with this orange flavoured cream, and pile the meringues on an ashet to serve. Pass the Strawberry and Orange Compôte in a bowl, to spoon alongside the meringues.

Strawberry & Elderflower Jam

This is my favourite jam; the delicate flavour of the elderflower is very noticeable, and to eat it in the depths of winter brings a keen anticipation of summer. When making strawberry jam, I find that a few under-ripe fruit help the set. I also put in a handful of redcurrants, but this is not essential.

157

---

3 lb (1.4 kg) strawberries
3 lb (1.4 kg) granulated
*   sugar*
juice of 1 lemon

handful of redcurrants,
*   stalks removed*
3–4 handfuls of elderflowers

Hull the strawberries, leave them whole and put them in a large saucepan or jam pan. Put the sugar in the pan, with the lemon juice and the redcurrants.

Carefully pull the tiny clusters of elderflowers off their stalks – do this over the saucepan, so that they fall into the pan. Add all the elderflowers to the pan. Cover the pan and leave in a warm place for a few hours; I put the pan in the bottom right-hand oven of my 4-door Aga for a couple of hours.

Then put the pan over a fairly gentle heat, stirring until the sugar has completely dissolved. Raise the heat, and boil furiously. After 10–15 minutes' fast boiling, remove the pan from the heat, and spoon a little of the juice on to a saucer. Leave this to get completely cold, then push the surface of the cold jam on the saucer very gently with the tip of your finger. If the jam wrinkles as you push it, your jam will set. If the jam on the saucer is still runny, put the pan back on the heat, and boil furiously for 5 minutes, then test again. Always take the pan off the heat while you are testing.

Leave the jam to cool in the pan for 20 minutes or so – then pour it into warmed jars. Cover with a waxed paper disc, and seal completely with cellophane and rubber bands when the jars are quite cold. There is nothing so satisfactory as popping into the larder to look at rows of home-made jam; I suppose I have a sort of squirrel complex.

August

In Scotland, the school summer holidays end in the middle of August, so the first half of the month we spend trying to make the most of the holidays. There are always friends and their children staying, which increases the holiday feeling in the house and spurs me on to make picnics for expeditions. Very occasionally we end up eating them round the kitchen table when the weather gets the upper hand, but it has to be deluging with rain for us to admit defeat. Here in Skye I look on The Weather as a definite opponent at such times.

With orange montbretia growing wild, Skye looks beautiful in August. During the month the hills turn colour as the heather comes into bloom. But autumn comes early in the north of Scotland and the trees begin to turn colour towards the end of August, and the bracken too begins to turn from dark, leathery green to its autumn hues of gold, bronze and copper.

Inevitably, once school goes back, we have a spell of lovely weather, usually the final really hot spell of the summer, the last time one can swim. After this, any good weather we have is tinged with an autumnal nip to the air, not conducive to removing clothes and rushing into the sea.

The garden produces a glut of delicious tomatoes, at its peak in August. What luxury it is to have such a quantity available. Courgettes are still abundant too, and truth to tell their appeal is on the wane, with Godfrey groaning at their appearance yet again – all very well for him, but I have to try and think of different ways of not only cooking them, but, dare I say it, using them up! There is a limit to the number of times courgettes can feature on the menu in the hotel.

Raspberries are plentiful throughout July and August. As with so many things, their ripeness and quality in our garden depends on the weather. Given a good spell of weather, we have pounds and pounds of them, and that, too, is a luxury, because there are some wonderful puddings to be made with raspberries, as well as jam. They freeze so well, too, just sealed in polythene bags.

First Courses

Tomato, Orange and Basil Soup
Cheese Puffs with Tomato Sauce
Avocado Pâté
Easy Cream Cheese Mousse
Fresh Herb Scones
Courgette and Mint Soup
Courgettes à la Greque

Picnic Food

Bacon and Cream Cheese Rolls
Cornish Pasties
Egg and Bacon Rolls
Beetroot and Orange Salad
Tarte Provençale
Salmon and Dill Cream Tart
Chicken with Pimento Mayonnaise

Desserts

Raspberries with Cinnamon Ice Cream
Raspberry and Peach Compôte
Cinnamon Pavlova with Raspberries and Cream
Raspberry, Hazelnut and Cinnamon Tart

Preserves

Raspberry Jam

Tomato, Orange & Basil Soup

When tomatoes are plentiful and cheaper to buy, even if
you don't grow your own, this is a lovely soup. It is good
served cold and best made with fresh basil, my favourite of
herbs.

Serves 6

---

1 lb (500 g) tomatoes
2 oz (50 g) butter
2 medium-sized onions,
peeled and chopped
1 stick of celery, sliced
1 large potato, peeled and
chopped
a few strips of orange rind
a few sprigs of fresh basil,

or ½ rounded teaspoon
dried basil
1¼ pints (700 ml) chicken
stock
¼ pint (150 ml) fresh
orange juice
salt and freshly ground black
pepper
½ rounded teaspoon sugar
6 tablespoons single cream

Cut the tomatoes in half – don't bother to skin them, the
soup will be puréed and sieved – but scoop out as many of
the seeds as possible. If left in, they tend to make the soup
bitter. Melt the butter in a saucepan and add the chopped
onion, celery and potato. Cook over a gentle heat for about
10 minutes, until the onion is soft and transparent. Stir
from time to time, to prevent the potato from sticking.

Add the strips of orange rind to the saucepan, and the
halved tomatoes. If you are using dried basil, add it now,
and pour on the chicken stock, fresh orange juice, salt,
pepper and sugar. Bring to simmering point, and simmer
gently for 30 minutes, or until the pieces of potato are soft.
Remove from the heat, and cool.

Purée the soup in a blender, together with the fresh basil.
Taste, check the seasoning, and sieve the soup into a bowl.
Keep it in the refrigerator until needed, and serve each

plateful of soup with a spoonful of cream swirled into the centre. Serve with Fresh Herb Scones.

Cheese Puffs with Tomato Sauce

These are delicious, deep-fried balls of melting cheese, with a crisp outside. They are not difficult to make, and loved by all who eat them. The tomato sauce is a good way of using up tomatoes and it freezes well, too.

Serves 4–6

2 egg whites	1 carrot, peeled and chopped
8 oz (250 g) Cheddar cheese, grated	1 stick celery, sliced
salt and freshly ground black pepper	1 clove of garlic, peeled and chopped
fresh white breadcrumbs	1 rounded tablespoon tomato purée
sunflower seed oil	a few sprigs of fresh basil and parsley
For the tomato sauce:	salt and freshly ground black pepper
1½ lb (700 g) tomatoes	
4 tablespoons olive oil	
2 onions, peeled and chopped	½ rounded teaspoon sugar

Make the sauce first. Cut the tomatoes in half, scoop out as many of the seeds as possible, and purée the tomatoes in a blender, or put them in a food processor, skins and all.

Heat the oil in a saucepan and add the chopped onions, carrot and celery. Cook over a gentle heat until the onions are soft and transparent. Add the chopped garlic, tomato purée, blended tomatoes, seasoning, basil, parsley and sugar. Simmer for 30–45 minutes, with the pan uncovered. As it simmers, the sauce will reduce. Remove from the heat, cool, then whizz in a blender and sieve it.

Whisk the egg whites to a froth, stir in the grated cheese

and seasoning to form a paste. Roll this cheese paste into even-sized balls, about the size of a walnut. Roll the cheese balls in the fresh breadcrumbs, and put the balls into the refrigerator for several hours.

If you don't have a deep frier, heat some oil in a saucepan, to a depth of about 2 in (5 cm). As you are only going to be cooking 3 of the cheese balls at a time, you needn't use a large saucepan. When the oil is really hot – test by dropping a piece of bread into it, the bread should sizzle – carefully put 2 or 3 balls into the oil, using a slotted spoon. Fry, turning them over, until golden brown all over. Don't be tempted to cook more than 2 or 3 at a time, because this reduces the temperature of the oil so that the breadcrumbs don't fry to a crisp quickly enough to seal in the cheese.

Keep them warm, on a dish with a couple of thicknesses of kitchen paper to drain off the excess grease. They keep warm perfectly well for about 30–45 minutes. Serve with warm tomato sauce.

Avocado Pâté

This delicious and easy pâté was concocted by Araminta Dallmeyer. It makes an excellent summer first course, either eaten on its own with toast, or stuffed with tomatoes, as in the recipe for Tomatoes Stuffed with Tuna Fish Pâté on page 141.

Serves 6

2 avocados	*2 rounded teaspoons tomato*
1 tablespoon lemon juice	*purée*
1 clove of garlic, peeled and	*3 oz (75 g) garlic and herb*
crushed	*cream cheese*
a few drops of Tabasco	

Cut the avocados in half, remove the stones, and scoop out their flesh into a bowl, scraping the insides of the skins to get as much of the flesh as possible. Mash and beat the avocado flesh, with the lemon juice and garlic. Add the Tabasco, tomato purée, and the cream cheese, combining all together until as smooth as possible. Or if you have a food processor, simply put everything into it, and whizz until you have a smooth purée.

Pile the pâté into a serving dish, cover with cling film and chill in the refrigerator. Serve with hot toast.

Easy Cream Cheese Mousse

There are two sorts of tinned beef consommé – you need the jellied sort for this recipe.

Serves 4–6

2 hard-boiled eggs, chopped, or 4 oz (125 g) shelled prawns, chopped	*1 clove of garlic, peeled*
6 oz (175 g) cream cheese	*1 rounded teaspoon curry powder*
15 oz (425 g) tin jellied consommé	*salt and freshly ground black pepper*
	parsley, to garnish

Divide the chopped hard-boiled eggs or prawns, whichever you are using, between 4 or 6 ramekins. Into a blender or food processor put the cream cheese, consommé, garlic, curry powder and a little salt and freshly ground pepper. Whizz until completely smooth then divide between the ramekins. Refrigerate until set. Decorate each ramekin with a small sprig of parsley.

Fresh Herb Scones

Use any herbs or just lots of finely chopped parsley.

Serves 6

---

12 oz (350 g) self-raising
  flour
½ rounded teaspoon salt
1 rounded teaspoon baking
  powder
1 egg, beaten

1 tablespoon sunflower seed
  oil
just less than ½ pint
  (300 ml) milk
3 rounded tablespoons finely
  chopped herbs, e.g.
  parsley, chives and fennel

Sieve the dry ingredients into a bowl and stir in the egg, oil, milk, and the herbs. Knead together well – it will be quite a sticky dough.

Pat the mixture out on a well-floured surface, to a thickness of about 1 in (2.5 cm). Cut the scones into 2½ in (6 cm) circles, and put them on a baking tray. Bake in a hot oven, 425°F (220°C) Gas Mark 7 (top right-hand oven in a 4-door Aga) for 10–15 minutes, until they are well risen and golden brown. Serve warm.

Courgette & Mint Soup

This soup is equally good served hot or cold.

Serves 6

---

2 oz (50 g) butter
2 medium-sized onions,
    peeled and chopped
2 lb (900 g) courgettes, with
    the ends cut off, chopped
    in chunks

2 pints (1.1 litres) chicken
    stock
2 handfuls of mint leaves,
    preferably apple mint
salt and freshly ground black
    pepper

Melt the butter in a saucepan and add the chopped onions. Cook over a gentle heat for about 10 minutes, until the onions are soft and transparent. Add the chopped courgettes and cook for another 5 minutes. Then pour on the chicken stock and add 1 handful of mint leaves. Cover the saucepan, and simmer for 30 minutes. Cool. Then purée the contents of the pan in a blender together with the remaining handful of mint leaves. Taste and season with a little salt and black pepper. Serve with Hot Cheesy Scones, see page 13.

Courgettes à la Greque

This recipe is good eaten hot or cold, it can be a first course or a vegetable accompaniment to a main course.

Serves 6–8

---

5 tablespoons olive oil
2 large onions, peeled and
thinly sliced
8 medium-sized courgettes

1 large clove of garlic, peeled
and finely chopped
1 lb (500 g) tomatoes
salt and freshly ground black
pepper

Heat the oil in a saucepan or deep frying pan. Add the thinly sliced onions and cook over a gentle heat until the onions are soft and transparent. Slice the courgettes, throwing away the ends, into pieces about $\frac{1}{2}$ in (1 cm) long. Add them to the onions in the pan, together with the finely chopped garlic.

Skin the tomatoes (see page 145), scoop out their seeds and roughly chop the flesh. Add the chopped tomatoes and the salt and freshly ground black pepper to the pan. Simmer gently for 45 minutes to 1 hour.

Bacon & Cream Cheese Rolls

Summer picnics, like barbecues, can be dressed up or down. When Alexandra, aged 9, was asked what her ideal picnic food was, she answered without hesitation 'sardine sandwiches and chocolate biscuits'. Personally, although I love both, I would add one or two other items. For mass family picnics, where the rule is that everything should be eaten in the fingers with no knives and forks involved, cold cooked sausages and pieces of chicken are universally appreciated. This simple, but delicious filling for brown rolls was introduced to us by April Strang Steel, and is now so enjoyed by our children that they ask for it as a sandwich filling for their birthday parties. It makes perfect picnic food.

Serves 6

---

4 bacon rashers
6 oz (175 g) cream cheese
1 clove garlic, peeled

1 rounded teaspoon tomato
purée, optional
6 brown rolls

Grill or fry the bacon rashers until well cooked and crisp. Drain and cool on kitchen paper, and put them into a food processor, if you have one, together with the cream cheese and clove of garlic. If you like, add the tomato purée too. Whizz until the bacon is broken up finely into the cream cheese and garlic mixture.

If you don't have a food processor, break up the bacon into very small pieces and put them into a bowl with the cream cheese. Chop and crush the clove of garlic, add it to the contents of the bowl, and pound and beat until the mixture is as smooth as possible. Divide evenly between the brown rolls.

Cornish Pasties

These make good picnic food, being extremely tasty and very filling. I use a cut of beef that my butcher calls rump steak. It is a lean braising steak that would be sold as topside or silverside in other parts of Britain.

Makes 4

---

shortcrust pastry, made with
   8 oz (250 g) flour
For the filling:
8 oz (250 g) lean braising
   steak
1 medium-sized onion,
   peeled and finely chopped

2 carrots, peeled and diced
2 potatoes, peeled and diced
salt and freshly ground black
   pepper
1 egg, beaten

Roll out the pastry and, using a small bowl as a marker, cut 4 circles out of the pastry about 6 in (15 cm) in diameter.

Cut the meat into small cubes. Mix together the cubed meat, chopped onions, and diced carrots and potatoes, and season with salt and freshly ground black pepper.

Divide the filling evenly between the circles of pastry, leaving about 1 in (2.5 cm) margin round the edge of the pastry circles. Dampen the edges of the pastry with water, and pinch them together tightly, forming a ridge down the centre of each pasty. Brush each with beaten egg, and put them on a baking tray. Cook in a hot oven, 400°F (200°C) Gas Mark 6 (top right-hand oven in a 4-door Aga) for 30 minutes, then in a lower oven, 350°F (180°C) Gas Mark 4 (bottom right-hand oven in a 4-door Aga) for another 45 minutes until a good golden brown.

Egg & Bacon Rolls

Serves 6

---

4 eggs	*salt and freshly ground black*
3–4 rashers bacon	*pepper*
2 tablespoons mayonnaise,	*a little shredded lettuce*
see page 128	*6 brown rolls*

Hard-boil the eggs. Grill or fry the bacon rashers until crisp, cool a bit, then snip with scissors into tiny bits. Shell the eggs when cold, and chop. In a bowl, mix together the chopped eggs, bits of bacon, mayonnaise and a little salt and pepper.

Cut the rolls in half and take some of the doughy middle out of each roll. Butter the rolls, put a little shredded lettuce on the bottom half of each, and divide the bacon and egg filling between them. Quite apart from being delicious, these rolls are very nutritious.

Beetroot & Orange Salad

Serves 6

---

6 medium-sized beetroot	*1 rounded tablespoon finely*
6 oranges	*chopped mixed parsley*
4 tablespoons French	*and chives*
dressing, see page 130	

Wash all the mud off the beetroot and trim off the tops. Don't peel them or they will 'bleed' into the water. Put them in a saucepan, cover with cold water and boil until tender (you should be able to push a skewer in under gentle pressure). Drain them and leave to cool. Skin them when cool enough to handle. Cut the cooked beetroot into fine, even-sized strips, about 1½ in (4 cm) long.

Cut the skins off the oranges, using a serrated knife and removing as much of the pith as possible. Cut between the membranes towards the centre of each orange, so that you have neat segments. Gently mix together the strips of beetroot and the orange segments with the French dressing, taking care not to break up the beetroot. Sprinkle the chopped parsley and chives over the top before serving.

Tarte Provençale

Serves 6–8

---

8 oz (250 g) shortcrust
   pastry
For the filling:
4 tablespoons olive oil
2 onions, peeled and chopped
1 carrot, peeled and chopped
1 stick celery, chopped
1 clove of garlic, peeled and
   chopped
1 rounded tablespoon tomato
   purée
1½ lb (700 g) tomatoes
a few sprigs of fresh basil or

½ rounded teaspoon dried
   basil
salt and freshly ground black
   pepper
½ rounded teaspoon sugar
2 eggs
2 egg yolks
4 oz (125 g) Cheddar
   cheese, grated
a few black olives, stoned

Roll out the shortcrust pastry and use it to line a flan tin about 9 in (23 cm) in diameter. Put it in the refrigerator for 30 minutes then bake blind in a moderate oven, 350°F (180°C) Gas mark 4 (bottom right-hand oven in a 4-door Aga) until evenly cooked and golden brown.

Meanwhile, make a tomato sauce as a base for the filling. Heat the oil in a saucepan. Add the onions, carrot, celery and garlic and cook over a gentle heat for 10 minutes, until the onion is softening and looking transparent. Cut the tomatoes in half, and scoop out as many of the seeds as possible, whizz the flesh in a blender, then add to the saucepan, with the tomato purée, basil, salt, pepper and sugar. Simmer with the pan uncovered for 40–45 minutes, then cool, purée in a blender and sieve the sauce. Measure 1 pint (600 ml) of the tomato sauce (if there is any left over, it freezes well and makes a lovely sauce for grilled and fried savouries).

Beat together the egg yolks and stir them into the 1 pint (600 ml) tomato sauce until well mixed. Pour this mixture into the cooked pastry case, sprinkle over the grated cheese, and stud the surface with stoned black olives. Bake in a moderate oven, 350°F (180°C) Gas Mark 4 (bottom right-hand oven in a 4-door Aga), for about 25 minutes or until the surface of the tart is just firm to the touch, under the melted cheese. Eat cold or warm.

Salmon & Dill Cream Tart

I used to make this recipe using cooked left-over salmon. It was good, but inevitably the salmon was dry. Then Angela Fox, who cooked with us at Kinloch for three happy years, tried making it with raw salmon, and the result was marvellous.

Serves 6–8

8 oz (250 g) shortcrust pastry	1 pint (600 ml) single cream, or milk and cream mixed
1 lb (500 g) fresh salmon	salt and freshly ground black pepper
2 eggs	a few sprigs of dill
2 egg yolks	

Roll out the pastry and use it to line a flan dish about 9 in (23 cm) in diameter. Put it in the refrigerator for 30 minutes then bake blind in a moderate oven, 350°F (180°C) Gas Mark 4 (bottom right-hand oven in a 4-door Aga) until evenly cooked and golden brown.

Cut the salmon into 1 in (2.5 cm) cubes. Arrange them evenly over the base of the cooked pastry case. Beat together the eggs, yolks, and cream or cream and milk mixture. Season with a little salt and lots of freshly ground black pepper then pour this over the salmon. Tear the dill into bits and scatter over the top. Bake in a low oven, 325°F (170°C) Gas Mark 3 (bottom left-hand oven in a 4-door Aga), for 30 minutes, until the filling is just firm to the touch. This is nicest served warm, but still makes good cold food for an elegant picnic.

Chicken with Pimento Mayonnaise

This dish can either be taken as a rather smart picnic item, in a solid polythene container, or it can be the main course of a summer party. It is easy and delicious.

Serves 6

---

4 lb (1.8 kg) chicken
butter
salt and freshly ground black
*   pepper*
2 × 6½ oz (190 g) tins
*   pimentoes*
1 rounded tablespoon tomato
*   purée*
1 rounded teaspoon sugar

1 large clove of garlic, peeled
½ pint (300 ml) home-made
*   mayonnaise, see page 128*
To garnish:
6½ oz (190 g) tin pimentoes,
*   drained and thinly sliced*
finely chopped parsley

Butter the chicken lightly and season it well. Place in a

roasting tin and roast in a moderate oven, 350°F (180°C) Gas Mark 4 (bottom right-hand oven in a 4-door Aga) for about 1 hour. Test to see if it is cooked by stabbing the thigh with the point of a sharp knife – the juices should run clear. If they are still pinkish, cook for a little longer. Remove from the oven and leave until cold. Cut the cooked chicken off the bones, cutting it into pieces as neatly as possible.

Put the pimentoes into a saucepan with a little of the water from the tin, and with the tomato purée, sugar, salt and black pepper. Simmer gently for 5 minutes. Cool. Purée in a blender together with the clove of garlic. Stir together the puréed pimentoes and the mayonnaise.

Arrange the cut-up chicken on a flat plate and coat with the pimento mayonnaise. Garnish with strips of sliced pimento, and sprinkle over the finely chopped parsley.

Raspberries with Cinnamon Ice Cream

Serves 6–8

½ pint (300 ml) double cream	1 rounded tablespoon ground cinnamon
4 eggs, separated	1½ lb (700 g) raspberries
4 oz (125 g) icing sugar, sieved	caster or icing sugar for the raspberries

To make the ice cream, whip the cream. Beat the egg yolks with 1 oz (25 g) of the sieved icing sugar until pale and thick, then beat in the ground cinnamon. Stir this mixture into the whipped cream. Whisk the egg whites until fairly stiff, then whisk in gradually the remaining 3 oz (75 g) of sieved icing sugar. Fold this meringue into the cinnamon cream, and pour into a plastic container. Cover and freeze.

Pick over the raspberries, pile into a dish and dust with caster or icing sugar. Take the cinnamon-flavoured ice cream out of the deep freeze 20 minutes before serving. Scoop dollops of the ice cream into individual plates or dishes and spoon the raspberries over the top.

Raspberry & Peach Compôte

Raspberries and peaches make a delicious, light pud to have at the end of a rich dinner.

Serves 6

6 peaches	*2 rounded tablespoons caster*
1 lb (500 g) raspberries	*sugar*

Dip the peaches one at a time into a small saucepan of boiling water, for 30 seconds (no longer otherwise they begin to cook). Remove the skins, which will slip off easily. Cut the peaches into slices, cutting towards the stone, so that you have neat segments.

Pick over the raspberries and mix them in a bowl with the peach slices. Sprinkle over the caster sugar, and leave for several hours. The two fruits combined will make a good juice as they sit.

Cinnamon Pavlova with Raspberries & Cream

Serves 6

---

4 egg whites
8 oz (250 g) caster sugar
1 teaspoon vinegar
1 rounded teaspoon cornflour
1 rounded dessertspoon
  ground cinnamon

1 lb (500 g) raspberries
½ pint (300 ml) double
  cream
2 rounded tablespoons caster
  sugar

Whisk the egg whites and when fairly stiff whisk in the caster sugar, spoonful by spoonful. When the sugar has all been whisked in, pour in the vinegar, and sieve the cornflour and cinnamon together over the meringue mixture. Fold all together quickly and carefully.

Put a piece of siliconised paper on to a baking sheet, and spoon the pavlova mixture on to it. Shape it into a round or oval about 7 in (18 cm) in diameter, and hollow out the middle with the back of a metal spoon. Bake in a moderate oven, 350°F (180°C) Gas Mark 4 (bottom right-hand oven in a 4-door Aga) for 5 minutes, then lower the temperature to about 250°F (130°C) Gas Mark ½ (top left-hand oven in a 4-door Aga) and continue baking for a further hour. Remove from the oven, turn upside down on to a flat plate and peel the paper off. As it cools, the hollow will sink, so that although the pavlova is upside down to the way it cooked, you will still have an indentation.

Whip the cream, stir in the sugar, and carefully fold in the raspberries. When the pavlova is quite cold, pile the raspberries and cream on to it.

Raspberry, Hazelnut &
Cinnamon Tart

Serves 8

For the pastry:
*4 oz (125 g) butter, hard
from the refrigerator*
4 oz (125 g) plain flour
1 oz (25 g) icing sugar
*1 rounded tablespoon ground
cinnamon*
*2 oz (50 g) chopped
hazelnuts*

For the filling:
1 lb (500 g) raspberries
3 oz (75 g) sugar
*1 rounded tablespoon
arrowroot*
*½ pint (300 ml) double
cream, lightly whipped*

If you have a food processor, put in the butter, cut in pieces. Add the flour, icing sugar and cinnamon. Whizz until the mixture resembles fine breadcrumbs. Add the chopped hazelnuts and whizz for a second more, just enough to blend the nuts with the rest of the ingredients, but not long enough to pulverise them, because one of the attractions of this recipe is the contrasting crunch of the hazelnuts.

If you don't have a food processor, put the butter, cut in small pieces, together with all the rest of the ingredients, into a bowl. Using your fingertips, rub the butter in, until the mixture resembles breadcrumbs.

Press the mixture lightly into an 8–9 in (20–23 cm) flan dish, and put into the refrigerator for an hour. Bake in a moderate oven, 350°F (180°C) Gas Mark 4 (bottom right-hand oven in a 4-door Aga) for 30–40 minutes, until the pastry is golden brown.

Put the raspberries and sugar together in a saucepan, over a gentle heat. As the raspberries heat they will make juice. Heat gently until the sugar has dissolved completely. Put the arrowroot into a small bowl or cup, and mix to a

178

paste with a little cold water. Stir in a couple of spoonsful of the hot raspberry juice, then pour the contents of the bowl into the saucepan and cook, stirring, over a gentle heat until the sauce boils. As it boils, the raspberry sauce becomes clear. Remove it from the heat and leave to cool. When the sauce is cold, spoon it into the cooled flan. If you like, cover with the whipped cream, or serve the cream separately.

Raspberry Jam

I used to think my passion for raspberry jam and cheese scones was just an idiosyncrasy. Then I married Godfrey and discovered that he likes Marmite on chocolate digestive biscuits!

The smell of raspberry jam cooking is one of the best kitchen smells there is. If the fruit is as freshly picked as possible, and contains some slightly under-ripe berries, it will be easy to get a set. The less boiling the jam has the better, to keep that beautiful jewel translucency in colour, as well as a good, fresh flavour.

Makes 6 lb (2.7 kg)

---

3 lb (1.4 kg) raspberries   *3 lb (1.4 kg) granulated sugar*

Put the raspberries into a large saucepan or jam pan, and crush a few of the berries. Heat the pan gently, for 30 minutes or so; the juices will run from the raspberries. Meanwhile, warm the sugar. Tip it into a large bowl and put in a very low oven for about 20 minutes – this helps it to dissolve more quickly when you add it to the raspberries.

With the pan still on a fairly gentle heat, add the warmed sugar and cook without boiling until the sugar is completely dissolved. Then raise the heat under the pan, and boil furiously for 5 minutes. Pull the pan off the heat and spoon a few drops of the jam on to a saucer. Leave to go completely cold, then, using the tip of your finger, push the jam on the saucer; if the surface of the jam wrinkles slightly, your jam will set. If it is still runny, put the pan back over the heat, and boil fast for another few minutes before you test again. Always take the saucepan off the heat while you are testing for a set. Pot into warmed jars while still hot and cover each jar with a disc of waxed paper. Then when the jars are quite cold, seal with cellophane and rubber bands and label.

September

Living as far north as we do, September brings with it the first hint of autumn. It also brings, providing the weather isn't too wet, an abundance of blackberries, which we always call brambles. I love picking brambles, and throughout September my hands are scratched and stained red from bramble-picking expeditions.

September, again depending on the weather, provides us with lots of mushrooms and chanterelles, both of which we pick and use at Kinloch.

First Courses

Mushrooms in Garlic Butter
Potted Salmon with Lemon and Walnuts
Prawn and Orange Mayonnaise
Stilton, Onion and Parsley Soup

Main Courses

Osso Buco
Mushroom, Almond and Garlic Crust Pie
Jugged Hare with Forcemeat Balls
Devilled Seafood
Chicken in Mushroom and Cream Sauce

Desserts

Plum and Sour Cream Cinnamon Tart
Bramble Suèdoise
Bramble Syllabub
Bramble Sorbet
Bramble Mousse

Preserves

Bramble Jelly

Mushrooms in Garlic Butter

This is a useful dish because you can get it ready before you put the children to bed, and keep it warm until you are ready for dinner.

Serves 6

---

1 lb (500 g) mushrooms
6 oz (175 g) butter
2 cloves of garlic, peeled and very finely chopped
1 dessertspoon lemon juice
salt and freshly ground black pepper

a pinch of grated nutmeg
2 oz (50 g) fresh breadcrumbs, brown or white
2 rounded tablespoons finely chopped parsley, optional

Count an even number of mushrooms per head and put them in a buttered ovenproof dish. Or slice the mushrooms and divide them between shallow individual dishes. Cream the butter, add the chopped garlic and beat in the lemon juice, the salt, pepper, nutmeg, breadcrumbs and parsley. Cover the mushrooms as evenly as possible with the butter mixture and put in a fairly hot oven, 400°F (200°C) Gas Mark 6 (top right-hand oven in a 4-door Aga), for 7–10 minutes until the butter is melted and bubbling and the mushrooms are soft.

Serve with wholemeal rolls to mop up the garlic butter.

Potted Salmon with Lemon & Walnuts

The walnuts add a good crunch to the smoothness of this dish, and I think it is worth frying the walnuts in a little butter and salt.

Serves 6

---

5 oz (150 g) butter
½ small teaspoon salt
3 oz (75 g) walnuts, broken into bits
12 oz (350 g) cooked salmon, skinned and flaked from the bones

grated rind of 2 lemons
juice of 1 lemon
a pinch of grated nutmeg
freshly ground black pepper

Melt the butter in a saucepan. Pour off 4 oz (125 g) into a small bowl and leave to cool. To the 1 oz (25 g) remaining in the pan, add the salt and broken walnuts. Fry the nuts over a gentle to moderate heat for about 5 minutes, stirring them or shaking the saucepan from time to time. Tip them on to a double thickness of kitchen paper to cool.

Put the flaked salmon into a food processor. You can do this in a blender if you don't have a food processor, but it is quite hard work as you have to keep stopping and pushing the mixture down on to the blades. Add the grated lemon rind to the salmon, and whizz. Then add the lemon juice and whizz again. Then slowly add the cooled melted butter, until it is all blended into salmon purée. Season with the nutmeg and black pepper. Stir in the fried walnut bits – don't whizz them, as they will be broken down by the blades, and the pâté will lose its contrast in textures.

Divide the salmon mixture between 6 ramekins, or alternatively heap into a single serving dish, and serve with brown toast.

Prawn & Orange Mayonnaise

The combination of prawns and oranges sounds unlikely, but is delicious. It is a refreshing first course, less filling than prawns by themselves tend to be.

Serves 6

---

4 oranges
¼ pint (150 ml) double
   cream, whipped
4 tablespoons mayonnaise,
   see page 128
1 clove of garlic, peeled and
   very finely chopped

1 tablespoon lemon juice
freshly ground black pepper
8 oz (250 g) peeled, cooked
   prawns
1 rounded tablespoon finely
   chopped parsley

Cut the peel off the oranges with a serrated knife, removing as much of the white pith as possible. Cut them into segments, cutting between the membranes towards the centre of each orange. Put the orange segments into a bowl, until you are ready for them.

In another bowl, mix together the whipped cream, mayonnaise, garlic, lemon juice and black pepper then stir in the prawns. If you are getting the dish ready in advance, do not add the oranges yet, as the juice that oozes from them will make the creamy mayonnaise mixture too runny.

An hour or so before serving, add the oranges to the prawn mixture, combine well together, and divide the mixture between 6 plates, or ramekins. Sprinkle over each plateful a little finely chopped parsley, and serve with sliced brown bread and butter.

Stilton, Onion & Parsley Soup

Serves 6

2 oz (50 g) butter
3 onions, peeled and thinly
  sliced
2 rounded tablespoons plain
  flour
2 pints (1.1 litres) chicken
  stock
6 oz (175 g) Stilton,
  crumbled

salt and freshly ground black
  pepper
a pinch of grated nutmeg
¼ pint (150 ml) single
  cream
2 rounded tablespoons finely
  chopped parsley

Melt the butter in a saucepan, add the onions and cook over a gentle heat, stirring from time to time, for about 10 minutes, until the onions are soft and transparent. Stir in the flour and cook for another couple of minutes. Then gradually add the chicken stock, stirring until the soup boils. Pull the saucepan off the heat and stir in the crumbled Stilton, stirring until it has melted. Season to your taste with a little salt, lots of black pepper and a pinch of nutmeg. You can make the soup to this stage in advance.

To serve, reheat the soup and just before serving stir in the cream and finely chopped parsley. If you add the parsley too soon, it will lose its bright fresh colour in the heat of the soup. Serve with warm brown rolls.

Osso Buco

It will take the butcher some time to saw up the veal, so if
you are in a hurry, tell him in advance what you want.

Serves 6

---

6 pieces of shin of veal,
    about 2 in (5 cm) in
    length
4 tablespoons olive oil
2 onions, peeled and thinly
    sliced
2 cloves of garlic, peeled and
    finely chopped
1 rounded tablespoon plain
    flour

2 × 15 oz (425 g) tins
    tomatoes
½ pint (300 ml) dry white
    wine
grated rind of 1 lemon
½ small teaspoon dried basil
salt and freshly ground black
    pepper
2 pinches of sugar

Heat the oil in a large flameproof casserole, and brown the
pieces of veal shin well all over. Remove them and keep
them warm. Add the onions to the fat and cook over a
gentle heat until they are soft and transparent, about 10
minutes. Add the garlic and flour, and stir all together.
Next add the tomatoes with all their juice, and the white
wine, stirring until the sauce boils. Stir in the grated lemon
rind, basil, salt, pepper and sugar. Replace the pieces of
veal shin in the casserole, keeping them upright so that the
marrow does not fall out of the bone during cooking.

Cover the casserole with a well-fitting lid and cook in a
moderate oven, 350°F (180°C) Gas Mark 4 (bottom right-
hand oven in a 4-door Aga) for 3 hours. The meat should
be nearly ready to fall from the bone. If you want to make
this in advance, cook for only 2 hours and reheat it, giving
it another hour in a moderate oven before serving.

Serve Osso Buco with boiled rice, to which you add the
grated rind of 1 lemon and 1 clove of garlic, chopped finely.

Mushroom, Almond & Garlic Crust Pie

This is a rather unusual pie, with breadcrumbs and almonds forming the crust instead of the usual pastry. I like to use nibbed or flaked almonds, as I like the contrasting crunch in texture. We do this as a first course at our Kinloch Hotel, but it can be quite filling, and makes a good lunch dish.

Serves 6

6 oz (175 g) wholemeal breadcrumbs
2–3 oz (50–75 g) nibbed or flaked almonds
pinch of dried thyme
2 cloves of garlic, peeled and very finely chopped
3 oz (75 g) butter, melted
For the filling:
2 oz (50 g) butter
8 oz (250 g) mushrooms, sliced

1 heaped tablespoon plain flour
just less than 1 pint (570 ml) milk
salt and freshly ground black pepper
pinch of grated nutmeg
2 egg yolks
1 rounded tablespoon finely chopped parsley, optional

Mix the breadcrumbs, almonds, thyme, garlic and melted butter together well, and lightly press round a 9 in (23 cm) flan dish. Bake in a hot oven, 400°F (200°C) Gas Mark 6 (top right-hand oven in a 4-door Aga), for 10–15 minutes, turning the dish round from time to time to brown it evenly. Remove from the oven when the surface feels just crisp.

Melt the butter in a saucepan, and add the sliced mushrooms. Cook for just 1 minute, then sprinkle on the flour. Stir well and gradually pour on the milk, stirring all the time until the sauce boils. Season with the salt, freshly ground black pepper and nutmeg (freshly grated if possible). Draw off the heat.

In a small bowl beat the egg yolks, pour a little of the mushroom sauce on to them, mix well, then add a little more sauce, mix well, then pour the contents of the bowl into the sauce in the saucepan and stir well. Pour into the flan dish, sprinkle with parsley, and bake in a moderate oven, 350°F (180°C) Gas Mark 4 (bottom right-hand oven in the Aga), for 10 minutes.

Jugged Hare with Forcemeat Balls

Hare is very good value for money. There is a great deal of meat on a hare, and it makes the most delicious, gamey dish when jugged. The sauce for jugged hare should be smooth and rich with the blood of the hare. If you are using a frozen hare and have no blood, put in more port than is given in the recipe.

Serves 6–8

---

1 hare, cut into joints
3 oz (75 g) butter
1 tablespoon sunflower seed oil
2 onions, each peeled and stuck with 4 or 5 cloves
2 carrots, peeled and roughly chopped
2 sticks of celery, chopped
1 bouquet garni
1 clove of garlic, peeled and chopped
2 strips of lemon rind
2 strips of orange rind
salt and freshly ground black pepper
For the forcemeat balls:
1 oz (25 g) butter
1 small onion, peeled and very finely chopped

4 oz (125 g) breadcrumbs
2 oz (50 g) shredded suet
1 rounded tablespoon finely chopped parsley
grated rind of 1 lemon
salt and freshly ground black pepper
1 egg, beaten
fat for frying
For the sauce:
stock from cooking the hare
2 oz (50 g) butter, softened
2 oz (50 g) plain flour
1 dessertspoon redcurrant jelly
¼ pint (150 ml) port
salt and freshly ground black pepper
as much blood collected from the hare as possible

Heat the butter and oil in a large, heavy, flameproof casserole which has a tightly fitting lid. Brown the pieces of hare thoroughly all over in the hot fat. Then remove the hare from the pan and keep warm. Add the prepared vegetables to the pan and cook over a gentle heat for 5 minutes. Replace the hare in the pan with the vegetables. Add the bouquet garni, the garlic, the strips of lemon and orange rind and salt and pepper. Cover the contents of the pan with water, put a piece of foil over the top of the casserole, and cover with the lid. Cook in a slow oven, 300°F (150°C) Gas Mark 2 (bottom left-hand oven in a 4-door Aga) for 3–4 hours, until the meat is tender and just beginning to come away from the bones. Remove from the heat and leave to cool in the stock.

Meanwhile, make the forcemeat balls. Melt the butter in a small saucepan, add the onion and cook gently until it is soft and transparent. Mix together the breadcrumbs, suet, parsley, grated lemon rind and seasoning. Stir in the cooked onion and bind together with the beaten egg. Roll into even-sized balls, about the size of a golf ball, and fry in fat, shallow or deep, until they are golden all over. Keep hot.

When the meat is cool, remove from the stock, strip from the bones, and put the meat in an ovenproof serving dish, while you make the sauce. Measure 1½ pints (850 ml) of the hare stock and put it in a saucepan over a gentle heat. Mix the butter and flour together well in a small bowl, then stir into it some of the hot stock; when thoroughly blended stir the contents of the bowl into the stock in the saucepan. Add the redcurrant jelly and stir continuously until the sauce boils. Stir in the port and the seasoning, remove the pan from the heat and pour a little of the hot sauce into the bowl with the blood. Mix well together, then pour this into the pan, and mix with the rest of the sauce. Reheat gently, adding extra stock if the sauce is too thick, but do not let it boil. Pour this sauce over the hare meat in the serving dish, and return to a low oven until the meat is reheated. Serve with forcemeat balls and redcurrant jelly.

Devilled Seafood

This was originally an American recipe which my mother brought home after we had lived in Norfolk, Virginia, for a spell when I was small. An American cup measures 8 fl oz (225 ml).

Serves 8

2 lb (900 g) fresh white haddock

1 lb (500 g) cooked shellfish, e.g. prawns, crab, scallops, lobster, or a mixture

8 oz (250 g) butter

9 rounded tablespoons plain flour

1½ cups fresh milk

1 cup evaporated milk

1 cup beef consommé

1 tablespoon lemon juice

1 tablespoon Worcestershire sauce

4 tablespoons tomato ketchup

1 tablespoon horseradish sauce

1 clove of garlic, peeled and very finely chopped

1 rounded teaspoon prepared mustard

1 rounded teaspoon salt

1 teaspoon soy sauce

¼ teaspoon cayenne

4 rounded tablespoons chopped parsley

¼ cup sherry

For finishing:
breadcrumbs
extra butter

Put the haddock in a saucepan with milk and water to cover. Bring slowly just to the boil. Remove from the heat. Cool, until cool enough to handle, then drain the fish and flake it into a bowl, removing all bones.

Melt the butter in a saucepan. Stir in the flour and cook for 2–3 minutes. Gradually add all the other ingredients, stirring until the sauce comes to the boil. When it has boiled, remove from the heat, and stir in the fish and shellfish. Butter an ovenproof dish, and pour the devilled seafood into it. Sprinkle breadcrumbs over the surface, dot with little bits of butter and reheat for 10 minutes under a medium-hot grill, to crisp the breadcrumbs. Serve with rice, and a green salad.

Chicken in Mushroom & Cream Sauce

Serves 6

9 boneless chicken fillets
2 oz (50 g) butter
2 cloves of garlic, peeled and very finely chopped
8 oz (250 g) mushrooms, sliced

1 level dessertspoon plain flour
½ pint (300 ml) double cream
1 tablespoon lemon juice
salt and freshly ground black pepper

Cut each chicken fillet in 3 pieces, lengthwise. Melt the butter in a wide frying pan. Warm a shallow ovenproof dish. Put the strips of chicken into the melted butter in the frying pan and cook over a gentle to medium heat, turning them, until they are cooked through. If you cook them on too fierce a heat, the chicken gets tough on the outside and the butter burns. Put the strips of chicken in the warm ovenproof dish, and keep warm.

Put the finely chopped garlic and the sliced mushrooms in the frying pan, and cook until the mushrooms are just soft. Sprinkle over the flour and cook for a couple of minutes. Stir in the cream and the lemon juice. Season with salt and pepper, and stir, with the sauce bubbling, for 3–4 minutes. Then pour the sauce over the cooked strips of chicken in the dish, and keep warm until you are ready to serve.

Plum & Sour Cream Cinnamon Tart

This is one of my favourite of all puddings. It features often on the menu at Kinloch, where it seems to go down well.

Serves 6–8

---

12 oz (350 g) shortcrust
  pastry
1 lb (500 g) plums
1 rounded teaspoon ground
  cinnamon
½ pint (300 ml) double
  cream
1 egg

3 egg yolks
juice of 1 lemon
4 oz (125 g) caster sugar
For the topping:
3 rounded tablespoons
  demerara sugar
1 rounded dessertspoon
  ground cinnamon

Roll out the pastry and line a flan dish about 9 in (23 cm) in diameter. Put in the refrigerator for 30 minutes then bake blind in a moderate oven, 350°F (180°C) Gas Mark 4 (bottom right-hand oven in a 4-door Aga) until evenly cooked and golden.

Cut the plums in half, then quarters, removing the stones. Lay the quartered plums evenly over the cooked pastry case. Sprinkle with the cinnamon. Mix together the double cream, egg, egg yolks, lemon juice and caster sugar, beating together until well mixed. Pour this over the plums, and bake in a moderate oven, 350°F (180°C) Gas Mark 4 (bottom right-hand oven in the Aga) for 30 minutes, until the custard part of the filling is just set to the touch. Remove from the oven. Mix together the demerara sugar and cinnamon for the topping, and sprinkle over the surface of the pie. Put it back into the oven for a further 10 minutes. Eat warm or cold, but I like it better served warm.

Bramble Suèdoise

A suèdoise can be made with any soft fruit, but is particularly good made with brambles, blackcurrants, or raspberries. It is also a useful pudding, because it can be made two or three days before it is needed. Keep it covered in its dish, before turning out, in the refrigerator. The meringues with which the finished suèdoise is covered can be made a couple of weeks ahead and kept in an air-tight tin.

Serves 8

For the meringues:
2 egg whites
4 oz (125 g) caster sugar
For the suèdoise:
2 lb (900 g) brambles
4–6 oz (125–175 g) caster sugar
½ oz (15 g) gelatine per 1 pint (600 ml) purée
½ pint (300 ml) double cream

To make the meringues, whisk the egg whites until stiff, then gradually whisk in the caster sugar. Cover 2 baking trays with siliconised paper and, using 2 teaspoons, shape about 24 meringues the size of a 10p piece. Bake in a low oven, 200°F (100°C) Gas Mark ¼ (top left-hand oven in a 4-door Aga) for about 3 hours, until firm and dry.

Cook the brambles without any extra liquid in a pan with a tightly fitting lid, over a very gentle heat until the juices begin to run from the berries. Cook until the brambles are just soft. Add 4 oz (125 g) sugar, stir until dissolved, taste, and add more sugar if you like. Purée the brambles in a blender and sieve, because the blender never breaks down the little wooden seeds in brambles or raspberries.

Measure the purée. To set the suèdoise you need ½ oz (15 g) gelatine for each 1 pint (600 ml) purée. For each ½ oz

(15 g) gelatine, put 3 tablespoons cold water in a small saucepan and sprinkle the gelatine on to it. Let it soak for a minute, then warm it very gently to dissolve the gelatine granules completely. Stir well into the bramble purée. Rinse out a bowl with cold water and pour the purée into the bowl. Leave to set, preferably overnight, in the refrigerator.

When you are ready to turn the suèdoise out, fill a bowl with hot water, dip a palette knife into the hot water and run it round the inside of the bowl. Holding the bowl of set purée tightly, plunge it into the hot water in the bowl for 1 minute (be careful not to let the water creep in). Take out, cover the top of the bowl with the serving dish and turn upside down. The suèdoise should fall neatly out of the bowl on to the serving dish. If it doesn't, turn it the right way up, and put it back in the hot water for another minute.

Whip the double cream until stiff and cover the suèdoise with whipped cream. Then cover the whipped cream with the tiny meringues.

Bramble Syllabub

Serves 6

---

2 lb (900 g) brambles	¾ pint (425 ml) double
4–6 oz (125–175 g) caster	cream
sugar or more according to	1 small wineglass dry white
taste	wine

Cook the brambles as in Bramble Suèdoise, (page 195). When the brambles are cooked, remove 6 whole berries from the pan and set them aside on a saucer, one for each glass of syllabub.

Purée the brambles in a blender then sieve them. Whip the double cream and white wine together. When the purée is quite cold, fold it together with the wine-flavoured cream, taste for sweetness and add more sugar if you think it needs it. Divide the creamy mixture evenly between 6 glasses. Put one bramble on top of each glass, and serve with homemade shortbread (page 212).

Bramble Sorbet

2 lb (900 g) brambles	*1 lb (450 g) caster sugar*

Put the brambles in a saucepan which has a tightly fitting lid and cook, covered, over a gentle heat until their juices run. Cool a bit and purée in a blender. Sieve the purée and leave it to cool completely.

In another saucepan put the caster sugar and 1 pint (600 ml) water. Place over a very gentle heat until the sugar is completely dissolved, then boil for $7\frac{1}{2}$ minutes. Remove from the heat and cool. Mix together the sugar syrup and the bramble purée, put into a hard polythene container, and freeze.

When it is frozen round the edges, and beginning to form crystals all through, remove from the deep freeze, and scoop the contents into a blender or food processor and blend. Refreeze. Repeat this as many times as you can – at least 3 times. The sorbet or water ice will become smooth, will never set hard because of the amount of sugar, and will always be easy to spoon out straight from the deep freeze.

Bramble Mousse

Brambles make a super mousse, providing you don't over-sweeten them; too much sugar detracts from the flavour.

Serves 8

---

1 lb (500 g) brambles	*1 oz (25 g) gelatine*
juice of 1 lemon	*½ pint (300 ml) double*
3 eggs, separated	*cream, whipped, but not*
5 oz (150 g) caster sugar	*too stiffly*

Cook the brambles in a saucepan with a tightly fitting lid, with the lemon juice. When the juices begin to run and the brambles are softened, remove from the heat. Leave to cool a little then purée in a blender and sieve the purée. Cool.

Put 3 tablespoons water in a small saucepan and sprinkle the gelatine in. Leave to soften a little then heat gently until the gelatine is dissolved. Leave to cool. Whisk the egg yolks and gradually add the caster sugar, whisking until they form a thick and pale-coloured mixture. Stir in the cooled bramble purée, and the dissolved gelatine.

Whisk the egg whites until very stiff. Fold the whipped cream into the bramble and egg yolk mixture, thoroughly blending them together, and lastly fold in the stiffly whisked egg whites. Pour into a bowl and chill to set. If you like, cover the surface of the mousse, when set, with more whipped cream.

Bramble Jelly

Bramble Jelly is so good it is tempting just to spoon it straight out of the jar into your mouth! It is so Scottish, and delicious on warm, buttery scones, or hot buttered toast. It makes a lovely present.

Put the brambles in a pan, and just cover them with water. If you haven't got too many brambles, you can pad out the quantities by adding some cored and roughly chopped apples which also help the setting. Simmer the fruit and water together until the fruit is really soft and disintegrating into the water. Remove from the heat, and have ready a large bowl, into which you strain the contents of the pan through a jelly bag or piece of muslin or cheesecloth. When as much juice as possible has been dripped and squeezed from the cloth, measure the liquid, and pour it into the rinsed-out saucepan. For each 1 pint (600 ml) add 1 lb (450 g) granulated or preserving sugar. Over a low heat, dissolve the sugar completely in the fruit juice, then bring to the boil and boil fast.

After 10 minutes' boiling, drop some on to a cold saucer, pull the pan off the heat while you wait for the jelly on the saucer to set. If when you push the liquid with your finger-tip the surface wrinkles, you have a set. If it does not wrinkle, replace the pan on the heat, and boil fast for a further few minutes and then test again. Using a small jug, or a ladle with a lip, pour the jelly into warmed jars, cover with waxed paper discs and seal with cellophane and rubber bands when cold.

October

Tea-time is a lovely time of day, with the children home from school and the curtains drawn against the darkness outside. And there is surely no country which produced better bakers than Scotland. The oven scones, pancakes (drop-scones to those south of the Border!), shortbread and fruit-cakes to be found in homes and bakers' shops all over Scotland are matchless.

Teas

Scottish Pancakes
Oven Scones
Fruit Cake
Chocolate Cake with Chocolate Fudge Icing
Gingerbread
Orange Cake
Vanilla Butter Cream Biscuits
Walnut Toffee Squares
Flapjacks
Brownies
Orange Biscuits
Real Scottish Shortbread
Swiss Roll
Chocolate Brandy Cake
Chocolate and Coffee Iced Eclairs
Profiteroles
Perfect Chocolate Sauce

Scottish Pancakes

Nearly every Scottish housewife has her own recipe for pancakes.

Makes 20—24

1¼ teacups plain flour	pinch of salt
¼ cup sugar	1 egg, beaten
½ rounded teaspoon bicarbonate of soda	½ large breakfast cup of milk
1 rounded teaspoon cream of tartar	oil for cooking

Sieve the dry ingredients together, and stir in the egg and milk until the mixture is well blended. If possible make up the batter in advance and leave it to sit for a few hours.

With my Aga, I lift the lid of the cooler hot plate about 20 minutes before I intend to make the pancakes, and oil the surface, then put spoonsful of the mixture on to the hot surface. When bubbles appear all over the surface of each pancake, they are ready to be turned over using a fish-slice or a large palette knife. If you don't have an Aga, use a griddle or large frying pan. They are best eaten still warm from the cooking. Pancakes will freeze well.

Oven Scones

This recipe is used by Peter Macpherson, who makes the scones freshly each morning at the hotel.

Makes 20–25

1½ lb (700 g) self-raising flour
1 rounded teaspoon salt
2 rounded teaspoons sugar, optional

2 rounded teaspoons baking powder
2 eggs
2 tablespoons sunflower seed oil
about ¾ pint (425 ml) milk

Sieve the dry ingredients together into a mixing bowl. Beat together the eggs and oil in a measuring jug and make up to 1 pint (600 ml) with milk. Stir the egg, oil and milk mixture into the dry ingredients. Knead (it will be fairly sticky), then pat the mixture out on a floured surface about 1 in (2.5 cm) thick. Cut out the scones with a 2½ in (6 cm) cutter. Bake in a hot oven, 425°F (220°C) Gas Mark 7 (top right-hand oven in a 4-door Aga) for 10–15 minutes.

These are best made and eaten the same day, but they freeze well. You can add some grated cheese to the basic recipe; to this quantity I would add 4 tablespoons grated cheese. Warm, buttery, cheese scones are delicious and go surprisingly well with jam, particularly strawberry, raspberry or blackberry jams.

Fruit Cake

This cake, like most fruit cakes, improves with keeping.

---

8 oz (225 g) butter
8 oz (225 g) caster sugar
10 oz (275 g) plain flour
4 large eggs, beaten
12 oz (350 g) raisins or
  sultanas
12 oz (350 g) currants

6 oz (175 g) mixed peel
4 oz (125 g) glacé cherries
4 oz (125 g) flaked
  almonds, toasted
grated rind of 1 lemon and
  juice of half the lemon

Prepare an 8 in (20 cm) cake tin by greasing it thoroughly, then shaking flour around to cover the inside. Cream the butter and sugar really well together, until they are fluffy and pale in colour. Sieve the flour, and sprinkle 2 tablespoons over the dried fruit; using your hands, mix the flour through the dried fruit so that it is evenly distributed. Gradually beat the eggs into the butter and sugar mixture, then stir in the flour, the dried fruit, mixed peel, glacé cherries, half the almonds and the lemon rind. Stir in the lemon juice. The mixture should be a soft, dropping consistency; if you feel it is too stiff, add more lemon juice.

Put the cake mixture into the prepared tin, arrange the rest of the almonds on the top, and bake in a moderate oven, 350°F (180°C) Gas Mark 4 (bottom right-hand oven in a 4-door Aga) for 30 minutes, then reduce the heat to 300°F (150°C) Gas Mark 2 (top left-hand oven in the Aga) and bake for a further 2 hours. Leave to cool in the tin.

Chocolate Cake with Chocolate Fudge Icing

No good tea-table is complete without a chocolate cake. This recipe exactly fills my bill for everything that a chocolate cake should be. It is very gooey, and very chocolatey. It keeps extremely well, and it is a most adaptable cake, because you can juggle around with the ingredients. If you would prefer an even stickier and rather fudgy cake, use dark soft brown sugar or, better still, muscovado sugar instead of caster sugar; and if you would prefer a less gooey and slightly less rich cake, use less drinking chocolate powder and more flour. It has the advantage of being very quick and easy to make, using only one bowl.

---

6 oz (175 g) butter
6 oz (175 g) caster sugar,
    dark brown or muscovado
    sugar
4 large eggs
8 oz (225 g) drinking
    chocolate powder
3 oz (75 g) self-raising flour
    (you can use plain, which
    gives an even stickier
    cake)
a few drops of vanilla
    essence

For the butter cream:
3 oz (75 g) butter
3 oz (75 g) icing sugar,
    sieved
a few drops of vanilla
    essence
For the chocolate fudge
    icing:
2 oz (50 g) butter
2 oz (50 g) granulated or
    caster sugar
6 oz (175 g) icing sugar
2 rounded tablespoons cocoa
    powder

Cream the butter and sugar well together, until they are light and fluffy. Add the eggs, one by one, beating really thoroughly in between. Sieve the flour and drinking chocolate together and add to the butter, sugar and egg mixture, and stir in a few drops of vanilla essence. The mixture will be fairly runny.

Grease and flour 2 sandwich cake tins, about 8–9 in (20–23 cm) in diameter, and divide the mixture between them. Bake in a moderate oven, 350°F (180°C) Gas Mark 4 (bottom right-hand oven in a 4-door Aga) for about 30 minutes, or until a skewer pushed into a cake comes out clean. Take out of the oven, and leave to cool in the tins for a few minutes, then turn out on to a cooling rack to cool completely.

To make the butter cream, beat together the butter and icing sugar until pale and flavour with a few drops of vanilla essence. Sandwich the cakes together with the vanilla butter cream.

Finally, make the icing. Put the butter, granulated or caster sugar and 6 tablespoons water in a small saucepan. Heat gently until the butter is melted and the sugar dissolved, then boil for 5 minutes. Sieve the icing sugar and cocoa powder together, pour on some of the liquid from the saucepan, and beat the icing really well, adding more liquid as you need it. As it cools, it becomes glossy. When it coats the back of the wooden spoon without running off, coat the cake with icing.

Decorate with walnut halves, or crystallised rose or violet petals, or with piped blobs of chocolate butter cream, which turns this cake into more of a gâteau, that can then be used as a pud for dinner.

Gingerbread

I like sultanas and bits of stem ginger in my gingerbread. This cake is best made several days before you want to eat it.

4 oz (125 g) butter	*8 oz (225 g) self-raising*
4 oz (125 g) soft dark	*flour*
brown sugar or, better	*1½ rounded teaspoons ground*
still, muscovado sugar	*ginger*
3 large eggs	*4 oz (125 g) sultanas*
8 fl oz (225 ml) black	*2 oz (50 g) ginger preserved*
treacle	*in syrup, drained and*
	chopped into bits

Cream the butter and sugar together until light and fluffy and beat in the eggs, one by one. Then beat in the treacle, the flour and ground ginger and stir in the sultanas and bits of preserved ginger. Grease and flour an 8 in (20 cm) round cake tin and spoon the mixture in. Bake for about 1 hour, in a slowish oven, 300°F (150°C) Gas Mark 2 (bottom right-hand oven in a 4-door Aga), until a skewer pushed into the cake comes out clean. Leave in the tin for 5–10 minutes then turn out on to a rack to finish cooling.

Orange Cake

A contrast to chocolate, and a great favourite at home, is an Orange Cake.

6 oz (175 g) butter	*6 oz (175 g) self-raising*
6 oz (175 g) caster sugar	*flour*
3 medium-sized eggs,	*grated rind of 2 oranges*
separated	*juice of 1 orange*

Prepare 2 sandwich cake tins 8–9 in (20–23 cm) in diameter, by greasing and flouring them. Cream the butter and sugar together until they are light and fluffy. Beat the egg yolks, one by one, into the creamed mixture, then fold in the sieved flour and grated orange rind, and stir in the orange juice. Lastly, whisk the egg whites until they are stiff, and fold them into the cake mixture.

Divide the mixture between the 2 tins, and bake in a moderate oven, 350°F (180°C) Gas Mark 4 (bottom right-hand oven in a 4-door Aga) for 20–30 minutes. The cakes are cooked when a skewer inserted into the middle comes out clean. Take out of the oven, and cool for a few minutes in the tins, then turn on to a cooling rack to cool completely. Fill with an orange-flavoured butter cream made by beating together 3 oz (75 g) each butter and sieved icing sugar and flavoured with the grated rind of 1 orange. Ice with a simple icing made from icing sugar beaten together with fresh orange juice.

Vanilla Butter Cream Biscuits

These biscuits are quick to make and are extremely popular with children.

Makes 8–10

---

4 oz (125 g) butter or margarine	*a few drops of vanilla essence*
2 oz (50 g) caster sugar	*6 oz (175 g) vanilla butter cream, see page 205*
5 oz (150 g) self-raising flour, sieved	

Cream the butter (or margarine) and sugar together well, then work in the sieved flour and the vanilla essence. Make the mixture into even balls, about the size of a large walnut. Put them on a lightly greased baking sheet, flattening the top of each with a fork. Bake in a moderate oven, 350°F (180°C) Gas Mark 4 (bottom right-hand oven in a 4-door Aga) for 15–20 minutes. Cool on a rack and sandwich together in pairs with the vanilla-flavoured butter cream.

Walnut Toffee Squares

These are very easy to make, and quite delicious if you like nuts. You can do the whole recipe in a food processor, if you have one, or a mixer using the dough hook.

Makes 12

For the base:
4 oz (125 g) butter, straight from the refrigerator
6 oz (175 g) plain flour
2 oz (50 g) brown sugar
For the top:
2 large eggs
2 rounded teaspoons ground cinnamon

3 oz (75 g) desiccated coconut
4 oz (125 g) broken walnuts
½ teaspoon vanilla essence
6 oz (175 g) brown sugar
½ teaspoon baking powder
a pinch of salt

Put the base ingredients in the food processor and blend until it is like crumbs. Then press the mixture into a lightly greased 8 in (20 cm) tin. Bake in a moderate oven, 350°F (180°C) Gas Mark 4 (bottom right-hand oven in a 4-door Aga) for 15 minutes. Next mix together the remaining ingredients and spread on the top of the pastry. Cook for a further 15 minutes at the same temperature. Cool in the tin, and cut into squares.

Flapjacks

This recipe was given to me by Araminta Dallmeyer. When I arrive at the Dallmeyers' house around tea-time, I always make a bee-line for the biscuit tin in the hope of finding flapjacks within.

Makes 12

---

4 oz (125 g) butter
1 tablespoon golden syrup
4 oz (125 g) caster sugar
2 oz (50 g) oats

2 oz (50 g) self-raising flour
3 oz (75 g) cornflakes or rice krispies

Melt the butter and golden syrup together in a saucepan, then stir in the remaining ingredients. Spread the mixture about ½ in (1 cm) thick on to a greased baking tray, and bake for 15 minutes in a hot oven, 400°F (200°C) Gas Mark 6 (top right-hand oven in a 4-door Aga). Transfer to a rack to cool and cut into fingers before completely cold.

Brownies

A plateful of Brownies in this house vanishes like the proverbial snow off a dyke.

Makes 16

---

2 oz (50 g) butter
2 oz (50 g) plain dessert chocolate
6 oz (175 g) muscovado sugar

2 large eggs, beaten
4 oz (125 g) self-raising flour
1 oz (25 g) cocoa powder
2 oz (50 g) chopped walnuts

Melt the butter and chocolate together in a saucepan then add the other ingredients. Stir all together well and pour into a greased and floured 8 × 6 in (20 × 15 cm) tin. Bake in a moderate oven, 350°F (180°C) Gas Mark 4 (bottom right-hand oven in a 4-door Aga) for 15–20 minutes.

Cool in the tin, and cut into squares. Brownies are very good served with vanilla ice cream.

Orange Biscuits

A very easy biscuit recipe, but they are so delicious that it is advisable to double the recipe.

Makes about 14

• 4 oz (125 g) self-raising flour	1 large egg yolk
2½ oz (60 g) caster sugar	To finish:
3 oz (75 g) butter or margarine	1 egg white
grated rind of 1 orange	caster sugar
	4 oz (125 g) plain chocolate, optional

Sieve the flour with the sugar, and then rub in the butter (or margarine) until the mixture is like breadcrumbs. Add the orange rind, and then the egg, until the mixture is solid. Knead until smooth then roll out to about ¼ in (5 mm) thick. Cut into round biscuit shapes with a floured 2 in (5 cm) biscuit cutter.

Put the biscuits on a very lightly greased baking sheet. Brush each biscuit with a little white of egg and sprinkle with a very little caster sugar. Bake in a moderate oven, 350°F (180°C) Gas Mark 4 (bottom right-hand oven in a 4-door Aga) for 10–15 minutes until just turning golden brown. Before you lift them on to a rack, let them cool a bit on their baking sheet, as they tend to break if you remove them immediately.

The biscuits are delicious just like that, but sometimes I melt some plain chocolate in a bowl over hot water and, using a small palette knife, spread a little melted chocolate on one side of each orange biscuit, and make a wavy pattern in the chocolate using a fork.

Real Scottish Shortbread

No tea in a Scottish house would be complete without shortbread. Katharine Robertson, who works with us at Kinloch, makes the best.

---

1 lb (500 g) plain flour	*8 oz (250 g) semolina or*
8 oz (250 g) caster sugar	*ground rice*
	1 lb (500 g) butter

Mix all the dry ingredients together well, and rub in the butter with your fingertips. Press into a shallow 10 × 14 in (25 × 35 cm) tin. Prick all over with a fork, and bake in a slow oven, 300°F (150°C) Gas Mark 2 (top left-hand oven in a 4-door Aga) for about 1 hour or until a pale biscuit colour.

The Scots, who really do have the edge on all other nationalities when it comes to concocting sweet delicacies, sometimes take shortbread and turn it into everyone with a sweet tooth's idea of a dream come true. They cook the shortbread, then cover it completely with a layer of toffee; when the toffee has set, they spread a layer of melted chocolate all over the toffee, cut the end result into squares and call it Millionaire's Shortbread.

Swiss Roll

A plain Swiss roll, filled with either orange or lemon curd, is a great favourite with children.

---

2 oz (50 g) plain flour	*8 oz (225 g) caster sugar*
2 oz (50 g) cornflour	*12 oz (350 g) lemon or*
4 large eggs	*orange curd*

First, lightly grease a Swiss roll tin about 8×10 in (20×25 cm) and line it with siliconised paper.

Sieve the flour and cornflour together into a bowl. Whisk the eggs, gradually adding the sugar, and whisk until the mixture is really thick. When you swirl the mixture and it holds its shape, it is ready (full 5 minutes of whisking with an electric whisk). Very carefully fold in the sieved flours and pour into the prepared tin.

Bake in a moderately hot oven, 375°F (190°C) Gas Mark 5 (bottom right-hand oven in a 4-door Aga) for about 40 minutes. The sponge is cooked when it springs back if you push it with your finger, and is beginning to come away from the sides of the paper. Have ready another sheet of siliconised paper, sprinkled with caster sugar. When the cake is cooked, carefully tip it on to the new paper and peel off the paper it was cooked on. Spread lemon or orange curd all over the hot cake and roll up.

You can make endless variations, like spreading whipped cream and strawberry jam over, in which case roll up the cake and paper together so that the cake cools rolled up, then, when cool, unroll, spread with whipped cream and strawberry jam and re-roll.

Chocolate Brandy Cake

This cake is extremely rich, and can be used as a dinner party pudding. It can be made up to 5 days in advance, it keeps in the refrigerator and it also freezes well.

---

8 oz (225 g) butter
8 oz (225 g) dark chocolate
3 tablespoons brandy
8 oz (225 g) digestive
   biscuits crushed into
   crumbs

3 oz (75 g) walnuts, broken
   into bits
3 oz (75 g) glacé cherries,
   roughly chopped
2 large eggs
3 oz (75 g) caster sugar

Melt the butter and chocolate together in a saucepan over a gentle heat. Stir until well mixed, then cool. Add the brandy, the crushed biscuits, broken walnuts and chopped cherries. Whisk the eggs and sugar until really thick and pale and fold into the chocolate brandy mixture.

Line a 2 pint (1.1 litre) loaf tin with siliconised paper as neatly as possible – the tidier you cut the paper to line the tin, the neater the end product will be. Pour the chocolate brandy mixture into the prepared loaf tin, cover with cling film, and put into the refrigerator to set. When it is really hard, run a palette knife down the sides between the paper and the tin, turn the cake on to a plate, and peel off the paper. I like to lay walnut halves and halves of glacé cherries in rows on top.

Chocolate & Coffee Iced Eclairs

Makes 10–12

---

4 oz (125 g) butter, cut into
    pieces
5 oz (150 g) plain flour
4 large eggs, beaten
¾ pint double cream, stiffly
    whipped
caster sugar

finely grated rind of 1
    orange, optional
Chocolate Fudge Icing, see
    page 205

Put ½ pint (300 ml) water and the pieces of butter together in a saucepan, and melt the butter over a gentle heat. While it is melting, sieve the flour on to a piece of greaseproof paper, or into a small bowl – the idea is that when it is time to add the flour you do so with a rush, all at once. Raise the temperature under the liquid in the pan. As soon as it boils, remove from the heat and as fast as possible add the flour. Beat hard with a wooden spoon for a minute or two until the mixture leaves the sides of the pan cleanly. (Beware – do not let the water and butter boil away merrily; as soon as it starts to bubble take the pan off the heat and add the flour.)

Switch from wooden spoon to electric beater, and add the beaten eggs bit by bit. The mixture should end up smooth and glossy when all the eggs are added. This all sounds a bit long-winded but so many people have said that they 'daren't' make choux pastry that I feel it is worth going into the making in minute detail, so that if you follow exactly what I say you simply can't go wrong!

Having got your glossy mixture in the saucepan, run a baking sheet under some cold water, shaking off any excess – you don't want your éclairs to sit in a puddle, but the steam created from a dampened baking sheet helps the éclairs to rise. Then, using 2 large teaspoons, put dollops of the choux pastry on the baking sheet, as evenly sized as you can. Or use a large piping bag and a wide star-shaped nozzle to pipe sausage-shapes, about 2½ in (6 cm) long, in rows not too close together, over the baking sheet. Bake in a hot oven, 425°F (220°C) Gas Mark 7 (top right-hand oven in a 4-door Aga) for about 25 minutes, or until they are firm and golden brown. Using a palette knife, remove them to a cooling rack.

You can freeze the éclairs, when cold, or keep them in an air-tight tin overnight. But do not fill them until shortly before you want to eat them, otherwise they tend to go soggy. Sweeten the whipped cream to taste with caster sugar and use it to fill the éclairs. The easiest way is with a piping bag with a small plain nozzle; poke a little hole with the nozzle and pipe in the cream through the hole. Otherwise cut a slit down one side and spoon the cream in.

If you like, add orange rind to the cream – this goes particularly well with chocolate-iced éclairs. Or melt the plain chocolate and let it cool, then stir it into the whipped cream – this is good with coffee-iced éclairs.

Ice the éclairs with chocolate fudge icing, or make up half the quantity with a coffee flavour. Substitute coffee powder for the cocoa; or if you have the coarse coffee granules, dissolve them in the liquid in the saucepan before adding to the icing sugar. I like to do an ashet of alternate coffee and chocolate iced éclairs.

Profiteroles

While we are on éclairs, use the same mixture to make about 16 profiteroles – 2 in (5 cm) round balls. Fill them with whipped cream, and pile them up in a pyramid on a round serving dish. Dust with icing sugar and serve with a chocolate sauce.

Perfect Chocolate Sauce

6 oz (175 g) sugar
7 fl oz (200 ml) boiling
   water
1 teaspoon vanilla essence

3 level tablespoons cocoa
   powder
2–3 oz (50–75 g) butter
3 tablespoons golden syrup

Put all the ingredients together in a saucepan, and dissolve
and melt together over a fairly gentle heat, then boil for 3
minutes. The longer you boil it, the thicker and fudgier the
sauce becomes; I find 3 minutes ideal, but certainly boil for
no more than 5 minutes, otherwise when it cools it is almost
solid. If the sauce is to be used for profiteroles, it benefits
from the addition of a couple of tablespoons of Cointreau,
or other orange liqueur. Chocolate sauce can be made in
advance and kept for several days in the refrigerator.

November

In November we begin to unwind after the season. It is generally a stormy month in Skye and we often have our first snow, just to remind us what winter holds in store. When it snows we go tobogganing in the fields, but I hate it when we have to get anywhere by road. Single-track roads (of which there are many on the island) mean that if you skid there is no choice but to slide straight into the peat bog at the side.

November is when I make my Christmas puddings and cake. If I was properly organized I would do them in October, but although my intentions are there each year, somehow I never quite get round to it. We are always stuck for a receptacle large enough to hold the ingredients for the Christmas puds for Kinloch, but one year we solved that problem by mixing them all up in the baby's bath. It is ideal for such things – Hugo has long since grown out of it and so now the baby's bath will undoubtedly become an integral part of the Kinloch kitchen equipment.

November also means game. Best of all I like my game plainly roasted, accompanied by game chips and bread sauce. But I am going to share with you some of the recipes with which we vary our game cooking both at home and in the hotel.

First Courses

Game Soup
Pears with Walnuts in Tarragon Cream
Cheese Sablés
Smoked Trout Pâté

Main Courses

Pheasant with Cream and Brandy
Pheasant with Fresh Ginger
Wild Duck Paprika
Wild Duck in Tomato and Orange Sauce
Braised Venison with Vegetables and Milk
Casseroled Venison with Pickled Walnuts

Vegetables

Beetroot Baked in Cream and Lemon
Sliced Potatoes and Onions Baked in Milk

Puddings

Mrs Hill's Christmas Pudding
Sailor's Duff
Pecan Pie

Cakes

Christmas Cake

Game Soup

This is a warming, delicious soup to drink in the winter. Years ago, I read in a recipe of Katie Stewart's the tip of putting a small amount of liver in game soup. Now I never make it without liver – it rounds off the flavour and the texture perfectly. The soup is made in two stages – first the stock, then the soup.

The stock is best made with uncooked birds, but more usually I find myself using cooked carcasses. Cut any cooked meat off and keep for the soup. A variety of carcasses is best – say, pheasant, duck and grouse – this is a good way of using up old grouse.

Serves 6

For the stock:
2–3 game bird carcasses
2 small onions, unpeeled, with half a dozen cloves stuck in each
2 carrots, peeled and roughly chopped
1 or 2 sticks of celery, chopped
a few strips of orange and lemon rind
bouquet garni
some black peppercorns
salt
For the soup:
2 oz (50 g) butter
2 rashers bacon, cut in bits

8 oz (225 g) game liver, trimmed and cut in bits
2 medium-sized onions, peeled and chopped
1 carrot, peeled and chopped
2 potatoes, peeled and chopped
1 clove of garlic, peeled and finely chopped
1 rounded tablespoon redcurrant jelly
2½ pints (1.4 litres) game stock
2 strips of orange rind
1 strip of lemon rind
salt and freshly ground black pepper
any left-over bits of cut-up cooked game
¼ pint (150 ml) port

Put the carcasses into a large saucepan, cover with water and add the rest of the stock ingredients. Bring the stock to the boil, then cover the pan tightly and simmer gently for 3 hours. Cool, and skim off any fat from the top. When quite cold, strain.

To make the soup, melt the butter in a saucepan. Add the chopped bacon and the pieces of trimmed liver. Cook over a moderate heat until the liver is cooked through, then remove the liver from the saucepan and keep on one side till later. Lower the heat under the saucepan and add the chopped vegetables and garlic. Cook gently, stirring from time to time, for 10 minutes.

Then stir in the redcurrant jelly, the stock, orange and lemon rinds and seasoning. Bring to the boil, cover with a lid, and simmer gently for 45 minutes, until the vegetables are soft. Remove from the heat and cool. When cold, purée the soup in a blender, adding the cooked liver and game meat to the soup as you purée it. Stir in the port and reheat.

Pears with Walnuts in Tarragon Cream

Serves 6

---

6 good-sized pears
lemon juice
2 eggs
4 rounded tablespoons caster
    sugar
4 tablespoons tarragon-
    flavoured vinegar
pinch of salt

½ pint (300 ml) double
    cream, whipped
4 oz (125 g) chopped
    walnuts

Peel the pears, cut in half, core, and brush each half at once with lemon juice to prevent browning.

Beat the eggs in a bowl, adding the caster sugar spoonful by spoonful. Beat in the vinegar and a pinch of salt. Beat until thick. At this stage you can keep the tarragon cream in a jar in the refrigerator for up to 10 days.

Fold the tarragon cream and the whipped cream together. Lay the pears, 2 halves per person, on plates with the flat side on the plate, and coat with the sauce. Sprinkle with the chopped walnuts.

This recipe is good served with Cheese Sablés, delicious little cheese biscuits.

Cheese Sablés

Serves 6

---

2 oz (50 g) butter	½ rounded teaspoon mustard
2 oz (50 g) plain flour	powder
2 oz (50 g) Cheddar cheese,	salt and freshly ground black
finely grated	pepper
	beaten egg

Rub the butter into the flour with your fingertips until the mixture is crumb-like. Mix in the grated cheese, mustard powder, salt and pepper, until the mixture is blended together into a dough. Roll out the dough about ¼ in (5 mm) thick on a floured surface, and cut into about 20 × 1½ in (4 cm) rounds with a scone cutter. Or cut in triangles about 1½ in (4 cm) across. Put the small shapes of rich cheese pastry on a baking tray, brush with a little beaten egg, and bake in a fairly hot oven, 375°F (190°C) Gas Mark 5 (top of the bottom right-hand oven in a 4-door Aga) for about 10 minutes until they are golden brown.

Leave the sablés to cool for 5 minutes or so on the baking tray, before you put them on a cooling rack, otherwise they tend to crumble and break easily.

Smoked Trout Pâté

I love all things smoked, particularly fish. But I don't think smoked trout freeze successfully for very long; they are fine for up to a month, but much more than that and the flavour goes on the decline. So, if you can, buy fresh smoked trout from a fishmonger you know.

Serves 6–8

---

4 small smoked trout
8 oz (225 g) cream cheese
juice of 1 lemon (or more, if you like)

plenty of freshly ground black pepper
1 rounded tablespoon finely chopped parsley, optional

Carefully skin the trout, and lift the flesh from the bones, removing as many bones as you possibly can.

Put the trout flesh and cream cheese in a food processor, and whizz until smooth and well mixed. Pour in the lemon juice, and add the freshly ground black pepper and the finely chopped parsley. Whizz again. Heap on to a serving dish and chill.

If you haven't got a food processor, put the cream cheese into a bowl and pound it, using the end of a rolling pin. Add the smoked trout flesh, and pound them together. Add the lemon juice, black pepper and parsley, and pound and mix all together.

Serve with hot brown toast.

Pheasant with Cream & Brandy

This is a lovely, extremely rich way of cooking pheasant.

Serves 6–8

---

2 pheasants
3 oz (75 g) butter
3 medium-sized onions,
　peeled and very thinly
　sliced
1 rounded tablespoon curry
　powder

2 rounded tablespoons plain
　flour
½ pint (300 ml) double
　cream
6 tablespoons brandy
salt and freshly ground black
　pepper

In a large, heavy flameproof casserole, which has a tightly fitting lid, melt the butter and brown the pheasants well all over. Remove from the pan and add the thinly sliced onions. Cook gently until the onions are soft, then replace the pheasants in the pan. Cover with a piece of foil and the lid, and put in a moderate oven, 350°F (180°C) Gas Mark 4 (bottom right-hand oven in a 4-door Aga) for 1 hour. Test to see if the pheasants are cooked by sticking the point of a sharp knife into the thigh; if the juices run clear and are not tinged with pink, the pheasant is cooked. If necessary cook a little longer.

Carve the pheasants and keep warm on a serving dish. Stir the curry powder and flour into the onions in the pan, and cook gently for 2–3 minutes. Stir in the cream and brandy and simmer, stirring, until the sauce thickens. Pour over the carved pheasant, and serve, with boiled rice.

Pheasant with Fresh Ginger

I went to great lengths to get fresh root ginger, once when I was away, and brought it home to experiment with. Only to find fresh root ginger both in the fruit and vegetable shed at Kinloch, from the wholesale greengrocers in Portree, and in Billy and Carol Currie's shop in Ardvasar, which just goes to show how adventurous our stockists and suppliers are here. This pheasant recipe is in contrast to the last, because it isn't rich at all.

Serves 6–8

---

2 pheasants
3 oz (75 g) butter
4 onions, peeled and thinly
    sliced
1 clove of garlic, peeled and
    finely chopped
1 piece of fresh ginger, about
    2 in (5 cm) long, cut in
    fine slivers
1 cooking apple and 3 sweet
    apples, all peeled, cored
    and chopped

1 rounded tablespoon plain
    flour
¾ pint (425 ml) dry cider
¾ pint (300 ml) game stock,
    or water and 1 chicken
    stock cube
salt and freshly ground black
    pepper

Melt the butter in a large flameproof casserole, which has a tightly fitting lid. Brown the pheasants really well all over, remove from the pan and keep warm. Lower the heat a little under the pan, and add the thinly sliced onions. Cook, stirring occasionally, until the onions are soft. Add the garlic, slivers of ginger, the chopped apples and the flour and cook for 1–2 minutes. Then gradually stir in the cider and stock, stirring until the sauce boils.

Replace the pheasants in the casserole and cover with

the lid. Cook in a moderate oven, 350°F (180°C) Gas Mark 4 (bottom right-hand oven in a 4-door Aga) for 1 hour. Test to see if the pheasants are done (see previous recipe). Take them out of the casserole, and carve. Put the carved pheasants into a serving dish, pour over the onion, ginger and apple sauce and serve.

Wild Duck Paprika

This recipe was given to me by my sister, Olivia Milburn.

Serves 4–6

2 wild duck (mallard)	1 rounded tablespoon plain flour
3 onions, peeled	
1 carrot, peeled and quartered	1 rounded tablespoon paprika
1 bouquet garni	1 rounded tablespoon redcurrant jelly
1 orange, quartered	
3 oz (75 g) butter	¼ pint (150 ml) red wine
1 clove of garlic, peeled and finely chopped	4 tablespoons sour cream
	salt and freshly ground black pepper

Put the ducks in a deep roasting tin. Pour water into the tin to come half-way up the inside. Put an onion, the carrot, bouquet garni and orange into the tin around the ducks. Cover the roasting tin with a double thickness of foil, and cook in a moderate oven, 350°F (180°C) Gas Mark 4 (bottom right-hand oven in a 4-door Aga) for 1½ hours. Remove from the oven, and cool.

When cold, remove the ducks from the stock, carve and put them on to an ovenproof serving dish. Slice the remaining onions. Melt the butter in a saucepan and add the sliced onions and the garlic. Cook gently for 15 minutes, stirring occasionally, until the onions are soft. Stir in the flour, cook for 1–2 minutes, then add the paprika, redcurrant jelly, red wine and 1 pint (600 ml) of the stock the duck cooked in. Stir until the sauce boils. Stir in the sour cream, salt and black pepper and pour over the duck in the serving dish. Cover the serving dish with either a lid or foil, and reheat in a moderate oven, 350°F (180°C) Gas Mark 4 (bottom right-hand oven in a 4-door Aga) for 45 minutes. The sauce should be bubbling.

Wild Duck in Tomato & Orange Sauce

There is a sweet and sourness to this sauce which goes well with duck.

Serves 6–8

2 wild duck (mallard)	*2 oz (50 g) plain flour*
1 onion, peeled and quartered	*¼ pint (150 ml) orange juice*
1 carrot, peeled and quartered	*2 oranges, peeled and chopped*
1 bouquet garni	*1 rounded dessertspoon redcurrant jelly*
For the sauce:	
2 oz (50 g) butter	*1 dessertspoon red wine vinegar*
2 medium-sized onions, peeled and thinly sliced	*salt and freshly ground black pepper*
1 rounded tablespoon tomato purée	

Put the ducks in a roasting tin with the onion, carrot and bouquet garni. Fill the tin half-full with water. Cover tightly with foil and cook in a moderate oven, 350°F (180°C) Gas Mark 4 (bottom right-hand oven in a 4-door Aga) for 1 hour or until the ducks are tender when tested with a knife. When the ducks are cooked, remove from the

oven. Strain the stock from the roasting tin and measure off
¾ pint (425 ml).

Melt the butter in a saucepan and add the sliced onions.
Cook gently until the onions are soft and transparent. Stir
in the tomato purée and the flour and cook for 1–2
minutes. Then gradually add the duck stock and orange
juice, stirring until the sauce boils. Add the chopped
oranges, redcurrant jelly, wine vinegar and seasoning to
the sauce; stir until the jelly is dissolved. Cut the ducks into
portions and place in an ovenproof serving dish. Pour the
sauce over, reheat in a moderate oven, 350°F (180°C) Gas
Mark 4 (bottom right-hand oven in the Aga), for about 20
minutes before serving.

Braised Venison with Vegetables and Milk

We get quite a lot of venison. In fact we get rather too much for my liking, for to tell the truth venison is not my favourite meat. It is a dry meat, relying on at least a couple of days' marinating for any moisture if it is to be roasted. But Peter Macpherson, who cooks with me at Kinloch, roasts venison to perfection, so that even I exclaim over it! This is how he does it.

---

a haunch of venison, about 10 lb (4.5 kg)
4 tablespoons sunflower seed oil
4 oz (125 g) butter
2 large onions, peeled and chopped
4 carrots, peeled and chopped
2 parsnips, peeled and chopped
4 leeks, washed and sliced
2 cloves of garlic, peeled and finely chopped
salt and freshly ground black pepper
1 pint (600 ml) milk
2 oz (50 g) plain flour

½ pint (300 ml) red wine
1 rounded tablespoon redcurrant jelly
For the marinade:
1 pint (600 ml) sunflower seed oil
2 onions, peeled and sliced
2 carrots, peeled and sliced
2 cloves of garlic, peeled and chopped
1 pint (600 ml) red wine
½ pint (300 ml) red wine vinegar
6 juniper berries, crushed with the end of a rolling pin
a bouquet garni

To make the marinade, heat the oil and brown the vegetables and garlic. Remove from the heat, and stir in all the other ingredients. Leave to go quite cold then pour over the venison, which should be in a deep dish. Cover and leave it marinating in a cool place for 2 days; baste the meat twice a day with the marinade.

When you are ready to cook, take the venison out of the marinade and pat it dry with kitchen paper. Heat the oil and 2 oz (50 g) butter in a roasting tin, and brown the venison well all over. Lift the haunch out of the roasting tin, and put all the prepared vegetables and the garlic into the tin. Season with salt and freshly ground black pepper, and put the meat on top of the vegetables. Put into a hot oven, 425°F (220°C) Gas Mark 7 (top right-hand oven in a 4-door Aga) for 30 minutes.

Remove the tin from the oven and pour the milk over the meat. Cover the tin with a double thickness of foil, wrapping it down around the edge of the tin tightly. Put in a low oven, 300°F (150°C) Gas Mark 2 (bottom of the bottom right-hand oven in a 4-door Aga) for 3 hours.

Remove from the oven, and put the venison on a dish to keep warm. Let the vegetables and the juices in the tin cool, then purée them in a blender. In a large saucepan melt the remaining butter. Stir in the flour and cook for 2 minutes. Stir the red wine into the flour and butter, bring to the boil, then stir in the puréed vegetables and the redcurrant jelly. Check the seasoning, adding a little more salt and pepper if you think it needs it. Carve the venison, and serve the sauce either poured over the slices, or handed round separately in a sauce boat.

Casseroled Venison with Pickled Walnuts

Years ago I used to do a stew with beef and pickled walnuts. Then it struck me that pickled walnuts might go just as well with venison, and they do. They seem to provide the sharpness and sweetness that venison needs.

Serves 6

2½ lb (1.1 kg) venison, cut into 1 in (2.5 cm) cubes
3 oz (75 g) beef or lamb dripping, or 2 oz (50 g) butter and 2 tablespoons oil
3 onions, peeled and thinly sliced
1 clove of garlic, peeled and finely chopped

2 rounded tablespoons plain flour
1½ pints (850 ml) stock
¼ pint (150 ml) red wine
15 oz (425 g) jar pickled walnuts, drained of their liquid
salt and freshly ground black pepper

Melt the fat in a flameproof casserole that has a tightly fitting lid. Fry the venison a little at a time, to brown it really well all over. As it browns, remove it from the casserole and keep warm. When all the meat is browned, put the sliced onions in the pan and, over a gentle heat, cook for 10 minutes until they are soft and transparent. Add the finely chopped garlic. Stir in the flour, cook for 1–2 minutes, then gradually add the stock and red wine, stirring until the sauce boils. Season with salt and black pepper, replace the venison in the casserole and add the pickled walnuts, put the lid on and put it in a moderate oven, 350°F (180°C) Gas Mark 4 (bottom right-hand oven in a 4-door Aga) for 1½ hours.

As with all casseroles, this is better made the day before it is required, and reheated. It is good served with a mixed purée of root vegetables such as celeriac and potato.

Beetroot Baked in Cream & Lemon

If you should happen to be counting calories, you can substitute natural yoghurt for the cream in this recipe. It will give a rather drier result, but is still good. Beetroot goes with all things gamey, and I think its spectacular colour dresses up the contents of a dinner plate like nothing else can.

Serves 6

---

2 lb (1 kg) cooked beetroot
grated rind of 1 lemon
¼ pint (150 ml) single
* cream*

salt and freshly ground black
* pepper*
2 rounded tablespoons
* breadcrumbs*

Butter a shallow ovenproof dish. Slice the cooked beetroot evenly about ⅛ in (3 mm) thick. Arrange the slices in the buttered dish, overlapping each other. Sprinkle the grated lemon rind over the beetroot. Pour over the cream and season with salt and black pepper. Bake in a moderate oven, 350°F (180°C) Gas Mark 4 (bottom right-hand oven in a 4-door Aga) for 20 minutes, then remove from the oven, sprinkle over the breadcrumbs, and put under a hot grill to toast the crumbs. This dish keeps warm very well for about 30 minutes.

Sliced Potatoes & Onions Baked in Milk

This way of cooking potatoes is very convenient, because you have to get it ready well in advance. It goes well with gamey dishes and meat stews or casseroles.

Serves 6

---

3 oz (75 g) butter
6 medium to large potatoes,
   peeled
3 onions, peeled

1 pint (600 ml) milk
salt and freshly ground black
   pepper

Use some of the butter to grease liberally a shallow, ovenproof dish. Slice the potatoes and onions as thinly as you possibly can, and as evenly as possible. Arrange the slices of potato and onion neatly in the dish, dotting with butter and seasoning with salt and black pepper as you go. Pour on enough milk to come just below the top of the potatoes, and bake in a low–moderate oven, 325°F (170°C) Gas Mark 3 (middle of the bottom right-hand oven in a 4-door Aga) for 1½ hours.

Mrs Hill's Christmas Pudding

This Christmas Pudding recipe has been used by our family for years. The Mrs Hill who originally gave it to my mother was the wife of a vicar in our village, Tunstall, many years ago. It contains no flour or breadcrumbs whatever, so the pudding isn't stodgy at all, and it isn't too sweet either.

Makes 1 large pudding

---

12 oz (350 g) shredded suet
12 oz (350 g) sultanas
12 oz (350 g) raisins, stoned and halved
6 oz (175 g) currants
6 oz (175 g) chopped candied peel

3 oz (75 g) flaked almonds – I like to toast mine first
grated rind of 1 lemon
½ rounded teaspoon freshly grated nutmeg
½ rounded teaspoon salt
6 eggs, well beaten
1 wineglass brandy
⅓ pint (200 ml) milk

Mix together all the ingredients, stirring well. Put the mixture into a 3 pint (1.7 litre) pudding basin or 2 smaller basins. Cover with a circle of greaseproof paper. If you have pudding basins with clip-on lids, just clip on the lid. Otherwise tie on a cloth and knot the corners on top so they don't trail in the water. Put the basin in a saucepan and half-fill with boiling water. Steam the pudding for 5–6 hours, taking care not to let the water in the saucepan boil dry. (This bit of advice comes from bitter experience – it's the sort of mistake one makes just once.) Keep the pudding in a cool place, ideally a larder.

To reheat the pudding on Christmas Day, steam again for 1½–2 hours.

Sailor's Duff

While we are on the subject of steamed puds, I can't resist putting in a recipe that comes from my American Aunt Janie. It has a lovely sauce that goes with it, and that goes well with Christmas Pudding, too.

Serves 6

---

2 egg whites
2 rounded tablespoons caster sugar
3 oz (75 g) muscovado sugar
1½ oz (40 g) butter, melted
1 rounded teaspoon bicarbonate of soda
7 oz (200 g) plain flour, sieved

½ rounded teaspoon baking powder
pinch of salt
For the sauce:
2 egg yolks
7 oz (200 g) icing sugar, sieved
½ teaspoon vanilla essence
½ pint (300 ml) double cream, whipped

Beat together the egg whites and caster sugar. Beat in the muscovado sugar and melted butter. Dissolve the bicarbonate of soda in 2 tablespoons warm water and beat into the mixture with the flour and baking powder. Lastly beat in 4 fl oz (125 ml) boiling water and a pinch of salt. Put into a buttered 2 pint (1.1 litre) pudding basin and cover with a circle of greaseproof paper. Clip on the lid or tie on a cloth (see Christmas Pudding). Put the basin in a saucepan, half-fill with boiling water and steam for 45 minutes. Then turn out on to a heated dish.

To make the sauce beat together the egg yolks, icing sugar and vanilla essence until pale and fluffy. Just before serving fold the whipped cream into the egg mixture.

Pecan Pie

You can make this heavenly pie with walnuts instead of pecans, but pecan nuts are now fairly widely available throughout this country. Godfrey and I first ate them on a visit to Texas several years ago. When we commented on how good were the pecans, with the accent on the first syllable of the word, we were gently corrected, and told that peecans were kept under beds; the right way to pronounce the name of the nuts was *pecarn*. Anyway, this pie is yummy.

Serves 8

12 oz (350 g) rich shortcrust pastry
4 oz (125 g) soft brown sugar
4 oz (125 g) butter, cut in bits
3 eggs, beaten
½ teaspoon vanilla essence
6 oz (175 g) golden syrup
6 oz (175 g) shelled pecans

Roll out the pastry to line a flan dish about 9 in (23 cm) in diameter. Put the dish into the refrigerator for 30 minutes then bake blind in a moderate oven, 350°F (180°C) Gas Mark 4 (bottom right-hand oven in a 4-door Aga). Remove from the oven when evenly cooked and golden brown, and cool.

Put the soft brown sugar, the butter, eggs, vanilla essence and golden syrup in a bowl. Put the bowl over a saucepan of gently simmering water and stir the contents until the sugar has dissolved and the butter melted. Take off the heat, stir in the nuts, and pour into the cooked pastry case. Bake in a moderate oven, 350°F (180°C) Gas Mark 4 (bottom right-hand oven in a 4-door Aga) for 20–30 minutes, until the filling is just firm to the touch. Remove from the oven, and serve warm or cold (I prefer it warm) with whipped but unsweetened cream.

Christmas Cake

This quantity makes a cake about 10 in (25 cm) in diameter

6 oz (175 g) chopped candied peel

6 oz (175 g) glacé cherries, chopped

6 oz (175 g) flaked almonds, toasted

1 lb (450 g) sultanas

1 lb (450 g) raisins

12 oz (350 g) currants

10 oz (275 g) plain flour, sieved

10 oz (275 g) butter

10 oz (275 g) soft brown sugar, light or dark, or muscovado

grated rind of 2 lemons and 1 orange

1 tablespoon black treacle

6 eggs, beaten

1 rounded teaspoon ground mixed spice

1 rounded teaspoon freshly grated nutmeg

2 rounded teaspoons ground cinnamon

1 wineglass brandy, sherry or whisky

Prepare a 10 in (25 cm) round cake tin, by buttering it then lining it with a double layer of siliconised paper. Either tie a double thickness of brown paper round the outside of the tin, or put the tin in a small cardboard box. Cut 2 circles of siliconised paper to go on top of the cake during cooking.

Prepare all the fruit – chop the cherries, toast the almonds (if you like, I love the flavour which comes from them through the cake), and put all the fruit and the almonds together in a bowl, with 2 rounded tablespoons of the flour. Using your hands, mix all together thoroughly, so that the fruit is evenly coated with flour.

Beat together the butter and the sugar, beating until they are fluffy, and paler in colour. Beat in the grated orange and lemon rinds and the black treacle. Beating all the time, add the eggs, a little at a time, adding some of the flour at the same time to prevent the mixture from curdling. Then mix in the rest of the flour, the spices and the brandy, sherry or whisky. Lastly, stir in the mixed fruit.

Put the cake mixture into the prepared tin, hollowing down the middle with the back of the wooden spoon. Put the 2 circles of siliconised paper on top of the cake, and put the cake into a moderate oven, 350°F (180°C) Gas Mark 4 (bottom right-hand oven in a 4-door Aga) for 20–30 minutes, then lower the heat to 275°F (140°C) Gas Mark 1 (bottom of the bottom right-hand oven in the Aga) and bake for 3 more hours. Test to see if the cake is cooked by pushing a skewer into the centre of the cake. If it comes out clean, the cake is cooked. Remove from the oven, and cool in the tin.

Have ready a double thickness of foil, and when the cake is cold, turn it out on to this foil which should be big enough to wrap completely round the cake. Before you wrap it up, stick a skewer into the cake all over, from top to bottom, and trickle some more brandy, sherry or whisky all over the cake. This part of the operation is purely optional, but it's what I do! Then wrap the cake up tightly, and store it in a cool larder until you are ready to marzipan and ice it.

December

Decembeer for me is geared almost entirely to Christmas. I love all the festivity and really enjoy the planning and preparations involved. I was amazed to read in a magazine article that in a list of twelve chief causes of stress in women, near the top of the list was Christmas. The answer, I am convinced, lies in being ahead of the game.

I make a rough menu plan, not just for the Day, but for the whole holiday. The centre of the whole thing is of course the turkey. I always order a fresh bird, which I can be sure will be full of flavour and texture. I like it to stretch to two meals over and above Christmas dinner, and with often as many as fifteen people in the house I have to order the largest I can fit into my oven, which is about 22 lb (10 kg).

Then I sort out those things which can be done well in advance, and preferably frozen. For Christmas dinner itself the stuffings and bread sauce can be frozen. For Boxing Day and the following days, I include plenty of soups and stews because amongst the rich traditional fare of Christmas a few plain dishes are more than welcome. So you will find that many of the recipes in this chapter have freezing instructions written in.

First Courses

Minestrone
Celery and Apple Soup
Tuna Fish Pâté-stuffed Eggs
Avocado with Spinach and Garlic Mayonnaise

Main Courses

Winter Navarin of Lamb
Roast Turkey
Lasagne
Irish Stew with Black Pudding
Fricassee of Turkey
Bread Sauce
Giblet Stock
Sausagemeat and Chestnut Stuffing
Lemon and Parsley Stuffing

Vegetables

Baked Stuffed Potatoes
Chicory and Orange Salad
Salad of Chinese Leaves

Desserts

A Proper Trifle
Egg Nog Cream Pie
Chocolate Roulade
Gâteau Diane

Preserves

Emma's Mincemeat

Minestrone

Serves 8

---

4 tablespoons olive oil
2 onions, peeled and chopped
8 rashers of bacon, cut in
    1 in (2.5 cm) bits
2 cloves of garlic, peeled and
    finely chopped
12 oz–1 lb (350–450 g)
    white cabbage, cut into
    thin strips
2 fairly large carrots, peeled
    and diced
2 potatoes, peeled and diced
4 sticks of celery, thinly
    sliced

½ pint (300 ml) red wine
2 × 15 oz (425 g) tins
    tomatoes
2 pints (1.1 litres) chicken
    stock
salt and freshly ground black
    pepper
½ rounded teaspoon sugar
½ rounded teaspoon dried
    basil
7 oz (200 g) tin baked beans
grated Parmesan cheese

In a large saucepan heat the oil. Add the chopped onion and bacon and cook gently for several minutes until the onion is soft and transparent, stirring from time to time. then add the garlic, the shredded cabbage, the diced carrots and potatoes and the celery, and cook for a further few minutes, stirring occasionally. Add the red wine, tomatoes, stock, seasoning, sugar and basil. Bring to a gentle simmer, cover with a tightly fitting lid, and cook on a low heat for about 1 hour.

At this point you can remove the pan from the heat, cool thoroughly, add the contents of the tin of baked beans, and freeze. If you are not freezing the soup, reheat it when you need it and serve with Parmesan cheese to sprinkle thickly on the top of each helping.

Celery & Apple Soup

The flavours of celery and apple combine well. The curry is optional. The soup has the advantage of being thickened only by the apples and so is good but satisfying for those who, if not exactly slimming, are trying to economise here and there on their calorie intake.

Serves 8

---

2 oz (50 g) butter, or margarine

2 large onions, peeled and chopped

3 medium to large cooking apples, peeled, cored and chopped

3 eating apples, cored and chopped, but with the skin left on

6 sticks of celery, chopped into 1 in (2.5 cm) pieces

1–2 cloves of garlic, peeled and chopped

1 rounded dessertspoon curry powder, optional, or more if you love curry

2½ pints (1.4 litres) chicken or vegetable stock

1 tablespoon lemon juice

salt and freshly ground black pepper

1 rounded teaspoon sugar, optional

Melt the butter or margarine in a large saucepan and add the chopped onion. Cook gently until the onion is soft and transparent. Add the chopped apples and celery, garlic and curry powder and cook for a further few minutes, stirring from time to time.

Pour in the stock and the lemon juice. Cover with a tightly fitting lid, and simmer very gently for about 45 minutes. Remove from the heat and cool. Purée in a blender and sieve to remove the stringy bits from the celery. Season to taste with salt, pepper and sugar if you wish (saccharine if you seriously are calorie counting) and either freeze, or reheat to serve.

Tuna Fish Pâté-stuffed Eggs

These stuffed eggs can be used as a first course, looking quite impressive but involving minimum effort. Or they can be the main part of a lunch dish, accompanied by salads. You can hard-boil the eggs in the morning, if you are planning the dish for dinner that evening; halve the eggs, keeping the whites in a bowl of cold water to prevent them from going tough. You can then make the filling, and 2–3 hours before dinner fill the egg halves.

Serves 6

---

6 eggs, hard-boiled	*lots of freshly ground black*
7 oz (200 g) tin tuna fish	*pepper*
6 oz (175 g) cream cheese	*a few black olives or some*
1 teaspoon anchovy essence	*finely chopped parsley, for*
a dash of Tabasco	*decoration*

Halve the hard-boiled eggs lengthwise and cut a tiny sliver off the bottom of each white half, so that they will sit securely. With the tip of a knife, gently ease the yolk out of each half, trying not to split the white.

If you have a food processor, put the yolks into it, add the tuna fish, cream cheese and seasonings. Whizz until the mixture is smooth. If you have no food processor, pound the ingredients together in a bowl, using the end of a rolling pin. Fit a piping bag, with a wide star-shaped nozzle and fill the piping bag with the mixture. Arrange the whites around a small flat plate or shallow dish, and pipe the filling into each hollow. When piping, try to follow the shape of the white, rather than making a tall blob in the hole. If you prefer fill the egg whites using 2 teaspoons, scooping the mixture with one, and pushing it into the white with the other. Decorate either by dusting the eggs with finely chopped parsley, or by putting a piece of black olive on each stuffed egg.

If you have used a sufficiently large dish, and have a space in the middle, you can fill this with shredded lettuce, or with tomato wedges.

Avocado with Spinach & Garlic Mayonnaise

You can make the sauce in the morning for dinner that evening.

Serves 6

---

3 large, ripe avocados
8 oz (225 g) frozen spinach,
  thawed and well drained
1 clove of garlic, peeled
1 tablespoon lemon juice

dash of Tabasco
6 tablespoons mayonnaise,
  either a good bought
  variety, or made as on
  page 128

This recipe is best made in a food processor. Put the spinach, with as much water squeezed out of it as possible, into the processor, together with the lemon juice, Tabasco and garlic. Whizz until you have a smooth spinach purée. Add the mayonnaise, and whizz again. Put this mixture into a bowl, cover with cling film, and put in the refrigerator until you are ready to use it.

A couple of hours before serving, cut the avocados in half, carefully easing out the stones with the tip of a knife – if they are ripe the stone will flick out easily. Peel off the skin and put each half, hole side downwards, on to individual plates. Spoon over the sauce, dividing it between each plate. If you like, a few prawns sprinkled on top of each avocado both tastes delicious and looks nice. Serve with warm brown rolls.

Winter Navarin of Lamb

This is a good dish to serve around Christmas time. A total contrast to turkey, it is a meal in one; that is, all the vegetables are cooked and served together with the meat, so you only need a green salad as an accompaniment. It will also freeze for a short time, 2–3 weeks, but if you are going to freeze it don't add the potato until you reheat it. This version of the classic Navarin recipe, which correctly made should have young and tiny spring vegetables in it, is delicious and adapts to the winter vegetables available at this time of year with no detriment to the end result.

Serves 8

---

3 lb (1.4 kg) boneless leg of lamb, trimmed and cut into 1 in (2.5 cm) cubes
3 rounded tablespoons plain flour
salt and freshly ground pepper
6 tablespoons sunflower seed oil
1 rounded tablespoon granulated sugar
15 oz (425 g) tin beef consommé, made up to 1½ pints (850 ml) with water
about 3 oz (75 g) tomato purée

2 cloves of garlic, peeled and finely chopped
2 sprigs of thyme, or a pinch of dried thyme
1 bay leaf
6 medium onions, peeled and cut into eighths
8 carrots, peeled and cut into fine strips about 2 in (5 cm) long
½ small turnip, peeled and cut into strips about the same size as the carrots
8–10 potatoes, peeled and cut into 1 in (2.5 cm) cubes

Season the flour with salt and pepper and toss the prepared meat in the seasoned flour, until it is all thoroughly coated. Heat the oil in a large flameproof casserole. Brown the meat, a few pieces at a time, in the hot fat, turning the pieces so that they brown really well all over. As you brown the pieces of lamb, bit by bit, sprinkle a little of the sugar over the meat in the pan. This improves not only the colour but also the taste of the dish. As the meat is browned remove it to another dish, and keep warm.

When you have browned the lot, pour the consommé and water into the pan, and stir in the tomato purée, garlic, thyme and bayleaf. Stir, scraping the meat bits off the bottom of the pan, until the liquid boils. Replace the meat in the pan, cover with a tightly fitting lid, and cook in a moderate oven, 350°F (180°C) Gas Mark 4 (bottom right-hand oven in a 4-door Aga) for 1 hour. Cool the casserole, and skim off any fat which forms on top.

While the casserole is cooling, prepare the vegetables. When the casserole is cool, add the vegetables, pushing them well down into the liquid. Add a little more water (or stock) if necessary. Put the casserole into a moderate oven, 350°F (180°C) Gas Mark 4 (bottom right-hand oven in a 4-door Aga) for 1 hour, or until the vegetables are cooked.

Roast Turkey

When it comes to getting the turkey ready for the oven, I like to get it stuffed and wrapped up on Christmas Eve, getting as much stuffing as possible into each end. I butter the bird liberally all over, season it with salt and freshly ground black pepper, and put it, bosom down, on a large piece of muslin. Then I wrap it up, and put it, still on its bosom, in a large roasting tin. This makes the breast deliciously moist, although it doesn't do much for the shape of the bird when cooked!

For a 22 lb (10 kg) turkey, put the bird in a hot oven, 400°F (200°C) Gas Mark 6 (top right-hand oven in a 4-door Aga) for an hour. Then turn the temperature down to 350°F (180°C) Gas Mark 4 (bottom right-hand oven in the

Aga) for 2½ hours. Then test it by sticking the point of a sharp knife into the thigh; the juices should run clear. If it is not cooked, put it back for another 30 minutes.

Lasagne

This is another good contrast to turkey, and one which you can make well in advance. Lasagne freezes beautifully and, like the navarin, is a whole meal in one dish, completed by a green salad.

Serves 6 or 8 less hungry

1 lb (500 g) lasagne (the sort you do not need to pre-boil)
2 rounded tablespoons grated Lancashire cheese
For the meat sauce:
6 tablespoons olive or sunflower seed oil
1½ lb (700 g) raw minced beef
8 oz (250 g) chicken livers, picked over and roughly chopped
4 rashers of unsmoked bacon, cut into thin slices
1 large onion, peeled and very finely chopped
1 or 2 (depends on your taste) cloves of garlic, peeled and very finely chopped
2 carrots, peeled and finely diced

1 stick of celery, finely sliced, optional
3 rounded tablespoons tomato purée
salt and freshly ground black pepper
½ rounded teaspoon dried basil
½ rounded teaspoon sugar
½ pint (300 ml) red wine
½ pint (300 ml) stock, or omit stock and use 1 pint (600 ml) wine
For the cheese sauce:
2 oz (50 g) butter
2 oz (50 g) plain flour
2 rounded teaspoons mustard powder
1 pint (570 ml) milk
4 oz (125 g) Lancashire cheese, grated
salt and freshly ground black pepper
a little freshly grated nutmeg

Heat the oil in a saucepan and brown the minced beef, bit by bit, until it is all really well browned. Keep it warm in a separate dish. Put the chicken livers in the hot oil until they are sealed all over – about 2 minutes. Remove, and add them to the minced beef. Lower the heat a bit and add the bacon, onion, garlic, carrots and celery, and cook gently for about 10 minutes, until the onion looks transparent. Stir in the tomato purée, salt and pepper, basil and sugar, the red wine and the stock. Replace the meat and chicken livers, and partially cover the pan with a lid. Cook, with the mixture barely simming, for an hour or so. The sauce should then be thick and smell and look delicious.

To make the cheese sauce, melt the butter in a saucepan and stir in the flour and mustard. Cook over gentle heat for 2–3 minutes, stirring, then gradually add the milk, stirring all the time until the sauce boils. Simmer for 1 minute then draw the saucepan off the heat and stir in the grated cheese, salt, pepper and nutmeg. Stir until the cheeese is melted.

In a large, shallow, ovenproof dish, layer the meat mixture, the pasta, and cheese sauce, until all is used up ending with a layer of cheese sauce. Sprinkle the top with grated cheese. When the dish is completely cold, cover it, and freeze. Thaw the night before you want to serve it, and bake in a moderate oven, 350°F (180°C) Gas Mark 4 (bottom right-hand oven in a 4-door Aga) for 1 hour, uncovered.

Irish Stew with Black Pudding

This recipe is not a proper Irish Stew, as it has black pudding in it. Perhaps we could rename it Scottish Irish Stew. It was my mother who made it with black pudding in, and urged me to try it; it was so good that now I always include it.

Serves 6

---

2 lb (900 g) neck of lamb, with as much fat trimmed off as possible
8 oz (250 g) black pudding, cut into small cubes
6 onions, peeled and sliced

6 carrots, peeled and either sliced or cut into fine strips
6 potatoes, peeled and sliced
salt and freshly ground black pepper

Layer up the prepared meat and vegetables in a casserole. Season with salt and pepper, and add enough water to just cover the meat and vegetables. Cover with a tightly fitting lid, and cook in a moderate oven, 350°F (180°C) Gas Mark 4 (bottom right-hand oven in a 4-door Aga) for at least 3 hours or until the meat is beginning to come away from the bones. Remove from the oven and leave to cool, preferably overnight. Skim off the fat from the surface. Cook for a further 1½ hours at the same temperature before serving.

Fricassee of Turkey

Serves 8

---

3 oz (75 g) turkey dripping or butter

2 onions, peeled and finely chopped

1 clove of garlic, peeled and finely chopped

2 leeks, sliced thinly, optional

6 rashers of bacon, preferably smoked, chopped

8 oz (250 g) mushrooms, wiped and sliced

1 scant dessertspoon curry powder

3 rounded tablespoons plain flour

1½ pints (850 ml) milk, or milk and stock mixed

1 glass of sherry

2 rounded tablespoons raisins

salt and freshly ground black pepper

1½–2 lb (700–900 g) cut-up left-over turkey meat

Melt the fat in a flameproof casserole and add the finely chopped onions and garlic, sliced leeks and bacon. Cook for about 10 minutes, stirring occasionally, until the onions and leeks are softened. Stir in the mushrooms, cook for 1–2 minutes then stir in the curry powder and flour. Cook for a further 1–2 minutes, stirring, then gradually add the milk, stirring until it boils. Let the sauce simmer very gently, stirring, for a couple of minutes. Add the sherry, the raisins and the seasoning. Cool the sauce, and when cold stir in the cut-up turkey meat. Reheat when you want to, simmering on top of the stove for about 20 minutes. Serve with garlic noodles, green or white, tossed in cream and a green salad.

Bread Sauce

Bread Sauce can be made several weeks in advance, frozen and forgotten about until Christmas Day. If you have a dish which is freezer- and over-proof, you can butter the dish well, pour the finished bread sauce into it, put dabs of butter over the surface, cover and freeze. The dish and its contents then only need to be thawed and reheated to serve. People's tastes vary when it comes to bread sauce – some think it an abomination to flavour it with cloves but personally I love it. I also feel very strongly that it must be made from a good, unsliced loaf. If it is made from a standard sliced loaf the sauce will be gluey.

Serves 6 (for people who love it)

---

1 large onion, stuck with cloves
1½ pints (850 ml) milk
8 oz (250 g) stale breadcrumbs, vary the quantity a little depending on how thick you like your sauce
2 oz (50 g) butter
salt and freshly ground black pepper

Put the clove-stuck onion in the milk in a saucepan, and put the pan on a very low heat for about 20 minutes, to infuse the milk with the flavour of the onion and cloves. Remove from the heat, cover and leave for an hour or so.

Stir in the breadcrumbs, cook gently for a few minutes then stir in the butter and seasoning. When the butter has thoroughly melted remove the onion and pour the bread sauce into a buttered serving dish. Cool thoroughly, cover and freeze.

Giblet Stock

Two days before Christmas I put the turkey giblets in a pan, fill it $\frac{2}{3}$ full of water, add a roughly chopped onion, skin and all (the skin gives the stock a good rich colour), a bouquet garni and a carrot chopped in 3–4 pieces. These are essential for the stock; if you can add a stick of celery too, and some parsley stalks, it will be even better. Cover the pan with a tightly fitting lid, and simmer very gently for as long as possible, 3 hours minimum, the longer the better. Cool, and when completely cold strain off the stock into a bowl or large jug and keep it in the refrigerator until you are ready to make the gravy on Christmas Day.

Sausagemeat & Chestnut Stuffing

This is a fairly large amount, enough for one end of a 22 lb (10 kg) turkey. Vary the quantities to suit your needs.

---

3 lb (1.4 kg) good pork sausagemeat
2 × 15 oz (425 g) tins unsweetened chestnut purée, or 2 tins whole chestnuts, unsweetened
4 oz (125 g) cashew nuts, optional
2 oz (50 g) butter

2 medium-sized onions, peeled and finely chopped
1 clove of garlic, peeled and finely chopped
½ rounded teaspoon mixed dried herbs
salt and freshly ground black pepper

In a bowl put the sausagemeat and the chestnuts, purée or whole. If you do use purée, you might like to add some cashew nuts; they give a good contrasting crunch.

In a saucepan melt the butter, and add the finely chopped onions and garlic. Cook gently, stirring from time to time, until the onions are softened and transparent. Remove from the heat and cool. When cool add the contents of the pan to the bowl of sausagemeat and chestnuts. Add the mixed herbs, a very little salt and lots of pepper and mix thoroughly. I find the only way to mix thoroughly is to use my hands – messy, but effective. Pack the lot into a polythene bag, label (it's frightening how anonymous things become when deep frozen) and freeze.

Lemon & Parsley Stuffing

Again, this is enough for one end of a 22 lb (10 kg) bird. Vary the quantities according to your requirements, but remember that you need twice the quantity of bread-crumbs to suet. Use a good unsliced loaf, rather than a sliced one.

---

2 lb (900 g) fresh white breadcrumbs
1 lb (450 g) shredded suet
4 oz (125 g) butter
2 large onions, peeled and very finely chopped
1 or 2 cloves of garlic, peeled and finely chopped

grated rind and juice of 2 lemons
2 eggs, beaten
4 rounded tablespoons (or more) very finely chopped parsley
salt and freshly ground black pepper

Mix together the breadcrumbs and suet in a bowl. Melt the butter in a saucepan. Add the finely chopped onions and garlic and cook gently until the onions are softened and transparent. Remove from the heat and cool. Add to the breadcrumb and suet mixture in the bowl, and stir in the parsley, salt and lots of pepper. The mixture may seem on the dry side, but don't be tempted to add more egg, because this makes the stuffing stodgy. When cool, pack into a polythene bag, label, and freeze.

Remember to take the stuffings out of the deep freeze the night before you want to stuff the bird – they need several hours to defrost.

Baked Stuffed Potatoes

These are extremely useful to have in the deep freeze for use during the Christmas holidays. They are good with cold roast turkey on Boxing Day, and it is lovely to just be able to pull them out of the deep freeze ready for reheating.

Serves 6

---

6 large potatoes, scrubbed
salt
2 oz (50 g) butter
2 egg yolks
4 oz (125 g) grated cheese

salt and freshly ground black
pepper
1–2 rounded tablespoons very
finely chopped parsley

Put the potatoes on a baking tray, and rub some salt into them. Cover (not tightly) with 2 butter papers, or a bit of lightly buttered foil. Bake in a moderate oven, 350°F (180°C) Gas Mark 4 (bottom right-hand oven in a 4-door Aga) for about 1 hour until the potatoes are soft. Remove from the oven and cool until you can hold them.

Cut each potato in half lengthwise and scoop out the contents with a teaspoon, into a bowl. Mash thoroughly until the potato is as smooth as possible, then beat in the butter, egg yolks, grated cheese, seasoning and parsley. If the grated cheese doesn't melt completely in the potato mixture, don't worry, it doesn't matter. Divide the potato mixture evenly between the 12 potato halves, and put them on a baking tray. When cold, put the baking tray in the deep freeze, until the stuffed potatoes are frozen hard. Then remove them from the deep freeze, put in a polythene bag, label, and refreeze. To serve they need 2–3 hours to defrost, then 30–40 minutes in a moderate oven, 350°F (180°C) Gas Mark 4 (bottom right-hand oven in a 4-door Aga).

Chicory & Orange Salad

When I refer to a 'green' salad as being a good accompaniment to a dish, I don't necessarily mean lettuce, which is usually expensive in December anyway. There are other salad alternatives which are much more widely available in the winter months. In particular I like chicory and Chinese leaves.

Serves 6

4 heads of chicory	*French dressing, or yoghurt*
3 oranges	*mayonnaise*

Separate the chicory leaves and cut them into pieces roughly 1 in (2.5 cm) long. Cut the skin off the oranges, using a serrated knife, and removing as much pith as possible. Cut the oranges into segments, cutting in between each membrane towards the centre of the orange. Mix together the orange segments and chicory, and dress with either French dressing or a mixture of equal quantities of plain yoghurt and mayonnaise.

Salad of Chinese Leaves

Chinese Leaves are wonderful, they keep very well in the 'fridge and can be used exactly as you would lettuce. Cut them up and dress with French dressing, or mix with other things, like tomatoes, or red peppers, to make a more colourful salad.

A Proper Trifle

Trifle has a bad reputation as being a sort of dustbin pudding, which indeed it is in some places. A proper trifle bears no relation to this whatsoever. The cake base should be a freshly made sponge, spread thickly with home-made jam. The cake and jam should then be liberally sprinkled with sherry. I liked sliced bananas next, but they are purely optional. What is essential is a proper egg custard.

Serves 6

---

1 round sponge cake	For the custard:
12 oz (350 g) strawberry or raspberry jam	*1 pint (570 ml) milk, or better still milk and single cream mixed*
1 wineglass sherry	
2 bananas, optional	*4 egg yolks*
½ pint (300 ml) double cream	*2 tablespoons caster or granulated sugar*
1 rounded tablespoon caster sugar	*1 rounded teaspoon cornflour*
toasted almonds to decorate	*a few drops of vanilla essence*

Spread the cake thickly with jam and put it in a wide, flat-bottomed dish. Sprinkle the sherry evenly over it and leave to soak while you make the custard.

Heat the milk in a saucepan until it is just beginning to form a skin. Beat the egg yolks, sugar, cornflour and vanilla essence together well, then pour on a little of the hot milk. Mix well, pour on a little more milk, then pour the egg yolk mixture into the pan with the rest of the milk. Over a very gentle heat stir until the custard thickens enough to coat the back of a wooden spoon. Do not let it boil. If it should look as if it is beginning to curdle, pour at once into a clean bowl and, as it cools, whisk with a rotary whisk; but it very rarely does curdle – the teaspoon of cornflour helps to prevent it.

Cool the custard. Peel and slice the bananas and spread them over the cake and jam then pour in the custard and leave until quite cool.

Whip the double cream, not too stiffly, and sweeten to your taste. Cover the top of the custard with the cream and sprinkle toasted almonds round the edges. If you prefer, glacé cherries and angelica look pretty, and Christmassy.

Egg Nog Cream Pie

This is a delicious creamy pie, with strong Christmas overtones. It freezes well, for a short period – 2 to 3 weeks. It is a particularly good pud to make and have ready in the deep freeze, if you are planning to have a party.

Serves 8

---

3 oz (75 g) butter, hard
  from the refrigerator
4 oz (125 g) plain flour
1 oz (25 g) icing sugar
For the filling:
½ oz (15 g) gelatine
½ pint (300 ml) milk
3 eggs, separated

4 oz (125 g) caster sugar
1 rounded teaspoon cornflour
1 level teaspoon freshly
  grated nutmeg
6 tablespoons rum
½ pint (300 ml) double
  cream, lightly whipped

Blend the butter, flour and icing sugar together in a food processor until they are well mixed and look like breadcrumbs, then press lightly into an 8–9 in (20–23 cm) flan dish. Place in the refrigerator for 30 minutes, then bake 'blind' in a moderate oven, 350°F (180°C) Gas Mark 4 (bottom right-hand oven in a 4-door Aga) until cooked and golden. Leave to cool.

Sprinkle the gelatine over 3 tablespoons cold water and

leave to soak. Heat the milk in a saucepan until it just begins to form a skin. Beat together in a bowl the egg yolks, caster sugar, cornflour and grated nutmeg. Pour a little of the hot milk on to the yolk mixture, stir well, then pour the contents of the bowl into the saucepan with the rest of the hot milk. Over a very gentle heat indeed, stir until the custard thickens enough to coat the back of the wooden spoon, but do not let it boil or it will curdle.

Remove from the heat and stir in the soaked gelatine; stir until the gelatine is completely dissolved in the hot custard, then stir in the rum. Leave the rum custard to get completely cold, when it will begin to set. Then gently stir in the whipped cream. Whisk the egg whites until stiff, fold them into the creamy rum custard, and pour the lot into the baked pastry case. Leave until set, freeze uncovered until the top is firm, then cover. It will take about 5–6 hours to defrost. Serve with grated chocolate sprinkled on top.

Chocolate Roulade

There are lots of versions of this roulade which is simple and quick to make and freezes beautifully. If you don't freeze it you can add sliced bananas and bits of preserved ginger to the whipped cream filling instead of the orange flavouring.

Serves 8–10

6 oz (175 g) dark chocolate
4 tablespoons black coffee or water
6 eggs, separated
6 oz (175 g) caster sugar
½ pint (300 ml) double cream, whipped

grated rind of 1 orange
1–2 tablespoons orange liqueur, e.g. Cointreau
1 tablespoon caster sugar
icing sugar for finishing

Line a Swiss roll tin about 10 × 8 in (25 × 20 cm) with a sheet of siliconised paper.

Melt the chocolate in the coffee or water in a bowl over a saucepan of simmering water. Whisk together the egg yolks, gradually adding the caster sugar, and whisking until they are thick and pale. Stir the melted chocolate into the yolk and sugar mixture. Whisk the whites stiffly, and using a metal spoon fold them into the yolk and chocolate mixture. Pour this into the lined tin and smooth it evenly into each corner. Bake in a moderate oven 350°F (180°C) Gas Mark 4 (bottom right-hand oven in a 4-door Aga) for 15 minutes or until firm to the touch. Remove from the oven and cover the roulade with a dampened tea-towel. Leave for several hours until completely cold.

Put a fresh piece of siliconised paper on a table or working surface and cover it with sieved icing sugar. Remove the tea-towel from the roulade and, gripping both your courage and each of the shorter sides of the roulade paper, turn it over, chocolate side down, on to the sugared paper. Carefully peel off the paper sticking to the roulade, in small strips. Instead of peeling the strips off vertically, peel them backwards parallel to the surface of the roulade; you will then have no trouble at all. This all sounds rather daunting, and something of a major operation, but please don't be put off because when you are actually doing it, it is dead easy.

Flavour the whipped cream with the grated orange rind, orange liqueur and caster sugar. Cover the surface of the roulade with the flavoured cream and, holding the siliconised paper, roll the roulade over lengthwise, on to a flat plate or serving dish. It will inevitably split a bit down the sides, but this doesn't matter. Cover, and freeze. Thaw for about 3 hours, and sprinkle with more sieved icing sugar before serving.

Gâteau Diane

This gâteau is ideal for a party. It has the bonus of being better for being made 1–2 days beforehand.

Serves 8–10

For the meringue:
4 egg whites
8 oz (225 g) caster sugar
1 level tablespoon instant
    coffee powder (not
    granules)
For the filling:
6 oz (175 g) unsalted butter

6 oz (175 g) icing sugar
3 egg yolks
3 oz (75 g) plain dessert
    chocolate
1 tablespoon strong black
    coffee
2 oz (50 g) grated chocolate
    for decoration

Whisk the egg whites and, when they are fairly stiff, gradually whisk in the caster sugar. Lastly, using a metal spoon, fold in the instant coffee powder. Put a layer of siliconised paper on a baking sheet, and mark two 7–8 in (18–20 cm) circles on the paper. Divide the meringue mixture between the circles and smooth evenly. Bake in a cool oven, 200°F (100°C) Gas Mark ¼ (top left-hand oven in a 4-door Aga) for 3 hours. Then remove from the oven, cool and carefully remove them from the paper.

Beat the butter, adding the icing sugar bit by bit, until the mixture is pale and fluffy. Beat in the egg yolks, one by one, beating well after adding each yolk. Put the chocolate, broken into bits, in a bowl with the coffee, and put the bowl over a saucepan of simmering water. When the chocolate has melted, remove from the heat, cool, then beat into the butter, sugar and yolk mixture.

Spread a layer of this butter cream on to one layer of meringue, put the other layer on top, and completely cover the top and sides with the remaining butter cream. Before serving, sprinkle with grated chocolate.

Emma's Mincemeat

Once you have used Emma Gillibrand's mincemeat for your mince pies, you will never again use bought mincemeat. It needs to be made 2 weeks before you make the mince pies, to mature, and it will keep for several months – but it begins to taste sour after much more than 9 months.

Makes 5½–6 lb (2.5–2.7 kg)

---

8 oz (250 g) seedless raisins
4 oz (125 g) chopped mixed peel
8 oz (250 g) sultanas
12 oz (375 g) currants
4 oz (125 g) chopped blanched almonds
1 lb (500 g) cooking apples, cored and chopped (leave the skins on)
1 lb (500 g) soft brown sugar

8 oz (250 g) shredded suet
1½ rounded teaspoons grated nutmeg
1 rounded teaspoon ground allspice
½ rounded teaspoon ground cinnamon
finely grated rind and juice of 1 orange
finely grated rind and juice of 1 lemon
6 tablespoons brandy or rum

Roughly chop (or put in a food processor for a second) the raisins, mixed peel and sultanas. Then stir in the currants, chopped almonds, chopped apples, sugar, suet, spices and orange and lemon rinds. Lastly stir in the orange and lemon juices and brandy or rum. (I prefer brandy.) Put into sealed containers, and keep for 2 weeks before using.

Index

Brown bread ice cream, 135–6
Brown garlic rolls, 143
Brown sugar meringues, 156–7
Brownies, 210–11

C

Cabbage fried with grainy
    mustard, 26
Cakes:
    Brownies, 210–11
    Carrot cake, 50–52
    Chocolate brandy cake, 214
    Chocolate cake with chocolate
        fudge icing, 205–6
    Chocolate and coffee iced
        éclairs, 215–16
    Christmas cake, 238–9
    Fruit cake, 204
    Gingerbread, 206–7
    Orange cake, 207–8
    Swiss roll, 213
Carrot:
    Carrot cake, 50–52
    Carrot and coriander soup,
        15–16
    Leek and carrot salad,
        100–101
    Parsnip and carrot ragout, 49
Celeriac mayonnaise, 40–41
Celery:
    Apple, chicory and celery salad
        with tarragon cream, 13
    Celery and apple soup, 244
Cheese. See also Cream cheese
    Cheese puffs with tomato
        sauce, 163–4
    Cheese sablés, 223
    Eggs with onion and cheese
        sauce, 62
    Ham, chicken and cheese
        salad, 125
    Hot cheesy scones with poppy
        seeds, 13–14
    Mixed cheese tart, 101–2

Cheese (*cont*)
    Mushroom, cheese and garlic
        soufflé, 45–6
    Scallops with white wine and
        cheese sauce, 67
    Spinach and cheese-stuffed
        pancakes, 99–100
    Stilton, onion and parsley
        soup, 186
    Stilton-stuffed pancakes with
        tomato sauce, 58–9
Cherry:
    Cherry and almond tart, 113–14
    Cherry and cream yoghurt
        pudding, 112
    Cherry jam and brandy sauce,
        112–13
    Chicken with fresh cherries in
        tarragon cream, 126
    Chocolate and cherry
        meringue gâteau, 114–15
Chestnut:
    Chocolate pancakes with
        chestnut cream and
        chocolate sauce, 71–2
    Sausagemeat and chestnut
        stuffing, 254–5
Chicken:
    Chicken and broccoli in
        mayonnaise cream sauce,
        85–6
    Chicken in curry mayonnaise,
        105–6
    Chicken with fresh cherries in
        tarragon cream, 126
    Chicken, leek and parsley pie,
        24–5
    Chicken in mushroom and
        cream sauce, 193
    Chicken with pimento
        mayonnaise, 174–5
    Chicken pizzaiola, 64–5
    Ham, chicken and cheese
        salad, 125